Lewis Morley was born in Hong Kong in 1925, the son of English and Chinese parents. He was interned in Stanley Internment Camp during the Japanese occupation between 1941 and 1945, when he was released and went to the United Kingdom with his family. He spent three years at Twickenham Art School, and lived in Paris as a painter in the early 1950s. His first published photographs were in *Photography Magazine* in 1957, followed by work in *The Tatler* in 1958, the beginning of a long association. In 1961 Lewis Morley Studios was founded at The Establishment in London. During the 1960s he took the first published photographs of Jean Shrimpton and Twiggy, as well as key portraits of Christine Keeler and Joe Orton.

Morley emigrated to Australia in 1971, where he worked from Studio Ben Eriksson. By 1972, he had opened his own studios in Surry Hills, often collaborating with Babette Hayes. His commercial work flourished in local style magazines until 1987, when he retired. In 1989 the National Portrait Gallery in London created an exhibition: *Lewis Morley: Photographer of the Sixties*, which is still touring the United Kingdom. A retrospective is planned for Australia in 1993.

BLACK AND WHITE LIES

BLACK AND WHITE LIES

SELF-EXPOSURES: SOME LONG, SOME SHORT, SOME INDECENT

LEWIS MORLEY

Angus&Robertson
An imprint of HarperCollins*Publishers*

CollinsAngus&Robertson Publishers' creative writing programme is assisted by the Australia Council, the federal government's arts advisory and support organisation.

AN ANGUS & ROBERTSON BOOK
An imprint of HarperCollinsPublishers

First published in Australia in 1992 by
CollinsAngus&Robertson Publishers Pty Limited (ACN 009 913 517)
A division of HarperCollinsPublishers (Australia) Pty Limited
25-31 Ryde Road, Pymble NSW 2073, Australia

HarperCollinsPublishers (New Zealand) Limited
31 View Road, Glenfield, Auckland 10, New Zealand

HarperCollinsPublishers Limited
77-85 Fulham Palace Road, London W6 8JB, United Kingdom

National Library of Australia
Cataloguing-in-Publication Data:

Morley, Lewis

Black and white lies

ISBN 0 207 17644 2

1. Morley, Lewis. 2. Photographs - Australia - Biography. I. Title.

779.092

Cover photograph: Self portrait with Christine Keeler *by Lewis Morley*
Typeset in Australia by Midland Typesetters, Maryborough
Printed in Australia by Griffin Paperbacks

5 4 3 2 1
95 94 93 92

This book is dedicated to the
THREE MEN, TWO LADIES AND A DAME
who made it possible

John Sloss
Shura Shihwarg
William Donaldson

Patricia Morley
Babette Hayes
Dame Edna Everage

My undying gratitude to

Lindsay Anderson
Elizabeth Butel
Colin Ford
Michele Field/Herbert Freudenheim
Horst and Sue Kolo
Robin Gibson—Terence Pepper
and
All those at the NPG

Not forgetting Tom who took a punt on uncharted waters

INTRODUCTION

It must be nearly thirty years ago now since I first met Lewis Morley. The brilliant young comedian, writer and impresario, Peter Cook, whom I had got to know in London, and later in New York, had invited me to perform at his new satirical club, The Establishment, in Soho. It was certainly the most insouciant and fashionable club in London in those far-off days. Its long corridor-like auditorium had been designed by Sean Kenny, whose sets for *Oliver* had, in a kind of tudor-constructivist style, been the sensation of the early sixties. Cook and his friends and satellites performed their squibs and pasquinades every evening, and later there was jazz and, perhaps, if one was lucky, a smoky song recital from Annie Rose with lyrics by Christopher Logue and music by Stanley Myers. The bar, which closed late, was a big attraction at The Establishment and was usually thronged with youthful satire enthusiasts eager for the latest impersonation of the Right Honourable Harold Macmillan or parodies of Hampstead earnestness. There were also a lot of pretty pale-faced girls in black with fringes, mascara'ed eyes and pearlised lipstick. They said 'yuh' a lot, and 'soopah'!

Over these premises were the offices of the long defunct *Scene Magazine*—overstaffed by the aforementioned kohl-eyed and fringed waifs—and a bare room sometimes used as a rehearsal room for the young satirists and at other times employed as a photographic studio. It was here that I was introduced to Lewis Morley, who had been commissioned by the club to take some portraits of me for front-of-house display in 1961.

A couple of days after my photographic session with Lewis I bumped into a thickset and extremely truculent young man called Jeffrey Barnard who insisted that *he* had been commissioned to take my photograph and that Lewis Morley had pinched his job. Barnard was not yet the famous, if desiccated, apologist for intemperance that he has subsequently become, but before our wary friendship developed, he could be an intimidating figure and I was somehow made to feel guilty that Morley had taken my picture and not he.

Throughout the sixties I saw much of Lewis Morley, who was always in black, as was the funereal fashion in those dufflecoated days before hippiedom. He was very tall, exotic and polite, and was a celebrity by 1963, having taken a famous photograph of Christine Keeler straddling a chair; an image that has been relentlessly imitated and pirated ever since. He was ubiquitous in the bars and clubs of Soho and at the parties of the *beau monde*, and his photographs were in all the glossy periodicals and in the display cabinets outside theatres from Shaftesbury Avenue to Sloane Square. I asked him to take some photographs at my house in Little Venice on the Regents Canal in Maida Vale and he wittily snapped me in 'aesthetic' postures on the sofa under my collection of lithographs of Charles Conder and reading an intriguing volume, picked up from a secondhand barrow, entitled *I Was Hitler's Maid*. Later in the sixties I bumped into Lewis again quite by accident during a holiday on the island of Cyprus. Again Lewis took photographs amongst the impressive Greek remains there.

I didn't see him again for many years, although once in the mid-seventies he came to see me in my dressing-room in Sydney. It had not occurred to me that he had made his home in Australia, even though his photographs appeared from time to time in Australian fashion magazines.

Two years ago, however, I 'rediscovered' my old friend in Sydney where he lived with his wife and an impressive collection of books and pictures. More than any other British photographer, Lewis Morley, it seems to me, has captured the spirit of his time. In the sixties he saw all of us, whether from the world of theatre, literature, music or fashion, with the detached eye of an outsider. This, coupled with his intelligence, humour and technical brilliance, has given us a gallery of portraits which is not merely an historical document but a poetic chronicle of an exciting age.

Barry Humphries
1992

BEGINNINGS

the American fiend... the New York connection...

As far back as I can remember, New York held a fascination for me. My Chinese grandmother had often spoken to me about the wicked city where my wicked grandfather had business and oft times visited, and the wicked white woman whom he had taken as a *Yee Nye*, a second wife. From what I could gather, he had actually married this *Fan Gwai Por*, foreign devil woman... the foreign fiend.

Grandmother was a very religious woman, and anything straying a centimetre from the straight and narrow was wicked. She was one of the old school, with the bound feet that denoted one who was not a labourer or a peasant. One who had to be looked after and had servants and therefore, money. In her late seventies, it was painful for her to hobble around on level ground and as we, at that time, lived on the first floor of a block of flats, she had to be carried up the two flights by our servants.

I remember peeping one day when she took off her little embroidered doll's shoes, exposing two terrifying lumps of compressed flesh and bones as she unwound the bandages that kept the mutilated feet in place. She gently caressed the misshapen toes and rubbed balm over the white crumpled flesh which seldom saw the light of day as she tried to ease the obvious pain that had resulted from her trip to our home. Then, they were squeezed back into the confining shoes that looked so dainty and innocent. It was the one and only time that I saw her performing this ritual and I was so horrified that I fled from the room each time she visited us and had to be dragged back in to greet her, after being promised that she wouldn't take her shoes off.

It was on these occasions that I questioned her about New York. She had never been there and could only reiterate some of the things her husband had told her. She spoke a different dialect to the one I had been brought up with in Hong Kong, and I could only get the gist of her ramblings. I tried to prise more information out of my mother but she always avoided the issue, saying I was too young to understand.

It wasn't until I was about twelve years old and my grandmother was dead, that my mother eventually told me what she knew of the matter, via an uncle who lived in *Gum San*, The Golden Mountain—San Francisco. On his frequent visits to New York on business, he had learnt the whole story from his brother.

According to him, my maternal grandfather, a mandarin in his own village, had business connections in New York and made frequent visits to fulfil these obligations. (The West has the idea that all mandarins are like the mandarin in *Turandot*, but there were all sorts of levels and often it signified only that the person in question was a bit better off than the rest of the village.) Aware of the Chinese proverb, 'Visitors are like fish, after three days they begin to stink' and the fact that his business sometimes stretched into weeks or even months, my grandfather considered that a second household, with a permanent housekeeper, was much cheaper and more convenient than the shuttling and ferrying of luggage between hotels, friends and relatives.

The housekeeper he chose was a perfectly respectable widow who had been married to a hard-working Irishman. The latter had succumbed to a heart attack after struggling with a piano and losing the battle on the second-floor landing, one flight from the cold-water flat where they were living after only three weeks of nuptial bliss.

Initially, my grandfather took her on purely as a favour to her brother, one of his business associates. It was to be a temporary measure until she recovered from the shock of her bereavement and found herself another job.

The weeks turned into months and they found that there was more to their relationship than just surface convenience. Perhaps her short marriage made my grandfather feel that the goods had not been too contaminated and this helped to counteract the fact that he was not marrying one of his kind. Chinese logic also deemed that a wife with her own house and the promise of a family with male offspring would be most desirable. He would gain prestige rather than loss of face, as he was saddled with a legal wife in China who had only female children.

As well, the installation of a cook, bottle-washer and bed-warmer of any nationality other than Chinese was less involved and expensive than having to engage the services of a traditional matchmaker, who would no doubt have someone in mind. Someone who might possibly come from the same village as him, thus letting the cat out of the bag to his wife at home. By taking advantage of a foreign devil he could make his own choice and perhaps indulge in the old adage of taste and try before you buy. I have a sneaking suspicion that my maternal grandfather had no intention of marrying initially, but with the addition of the male offspring, I feel certain that the white devil demanded respectability and the security brought about by matrimonial ties.

paradise lost...

In 1935, when I was ten years old, my father took overseas leave to England, taking the whole family with him—myself, my elder brother and my younger sister. On the ship going back to Hong Kong, there was an English family, whom we already knew, who were returning too. Their daughter, Maureen, was about three years older than me and was my friend.

We sported in the swimming pool, a cube of iron set into the top deck of the ship and open to the blazing blue sky. The water, which had been pumped in from the sea, soon matched the body's temperature and it was pleasant just to wallow in the swell that was made as other children and their parents leapt in or dived from the low springboard that jutted out from one side.

We clung to the railing that ran around the top of the pool, just above the surface of the water, very close to each other so as to hear ourselves speak above the screeches of the other children. Here we were content to steal furtive kisses on the cheek when we thought no one was looking.

Our bodies gently collided each time someone hurled themselves in, and each collision sent shudders of excitement through us, which were wordlessly conveyed each time our eyes met.

We were suddenly aware than the involuntary buffeting had ceased and a raucous voice was yelling at us to get out of the pool. It was then that we realised we were the only ones left and the Lascar deckhands were busy hauling a tarpaulin cover over the pool. 'Get out, get out!' they yelled, but we ignored them.

They left a corner uncovered for us to clamber out and departed for other duties. We stayed on, making the best of the seclusion to indulge in a little more cheek-pecking, oblivious to what was happening. Then our arms were much higher above us and we realised that they were draining the pool. We dog-paddled as the level dropped lower and lower. Soon it was completely empty and we found ourselves standing on the bottom of the pool, now quite dark, with the sun blocked out by the tarpaulin. The shaft of light that squeezed through the open corner, eerily illuminated the green, painted sides of the pool, the air warm with the midday sun.

It became very humid in the enclosed space, with the smell of rust and paint rising from the huge, now empty cube. Maureen pulled me across the pool into a corner and started to pull down my swimming trunks. I responded by clumsily trying to get my fingers under the tight opening of her costume. I was so inept that she helped me by pulling her costume aside for me to reach my goal. What bliss! I was breathless with excitement and the smell of the rusty paint was so overpowering that I felt I was going into a swoon.

Years later, the meaning of the term 'a kneetrembler' was fully understood, without having to be explained. I was on the point of physical, mental and moral collapse when I was rudely brought back to reality by gales of laughter. We looked up to the open corner and saw two or three turbanned heads, silhouetted against the blue sky, ice-cold compared with the burning red of my exposure.

In between the hilarity, instructions were yelled at us to climb up the ladder of iron rungs that ran up the side of the pool. Their comments were made in a language we couldn't understand, but the expressions on their faces and the gestures that accompanied them, conveyed their meaning much clearer than any words.

We prepared to face our expulsion from the riveted sheet-iron womb with as much dignity as we could muster and with lowered heads we made our way to the exit, expelled from Eden.

Maureen climbed up before me, her costume still pulled to one side but I averted my gaze now, mesmerised by the surface of the swimming pool which had bubbled and been repainted, time and time again at each eruption of rust caused by the sea water. Now it was like the skin of an unripe orange.

We left the pool, scurrying to our cabins, like a wedding couple to their get-away car, through an aisle of deckhands who had been brought to the scene of the crime by the loud guffaws of their compatriots.

All that was left of the escapade was a pattern of small wet footprints leading to the lower decks, drying rapidly in the sun.

Often when I peel an orange that still has vestiges of green on its mottled skin, bittersweet memories of sight, sound and smell return with varying intensities, tempered by the prevailing mood.

a fringe dweller...

In Hong Kong in 1940, a Eurasian was a little suspect. Hong Kong society was stratified, the principal layers being Chinese, Eurasian, Portuguese, and the Portuguese from Macau, the Meccanese. There was still the stigma of being of mixed race. It was acceptable for a European to have a Chinese mistress, but for a European woman to have a Chinese lover—my God!

My father was the chief pharmacist for the colony, which was fortunate for me socially. People might say, 'He's Eurasian, but his father's . . .'. I had a very cushy life, but being Eurasian wasn't all that easy. *What is he?* people thought. *Neither one thing nor the other.* One was made to feel ashamed and perhaps my whole attitude to life was affected by it.

I always felt more European than I did Chinese. My early days were spent in a purely English school where the only other student like me was half-Japanese, and I looked down upon him! The Japanese were *personae non gratae*, on a par with the Sikhs, in pre-war Hong Kong.

The Morley family in Hong Kong, 1927: (*from left*) Lewis John, C.H. (Peter), Lewis (Freddy) and mother Lucy.

My attitude was more European. When I was older and went to a mixed school, I found myself mixing more with the Europeans. I didn't really have Chinese friends. Their way of life was not my way of life, although in later years I have realised that many of my intrinsic attitudes are very Chinese.

The half of me that was Chinese was always governed by restrictions. The fact that you knew you would not get a certain job because you were Chinese; that if you could get anywhere it would be through the European side. One tends to lean towards whichever side is in power. But finally I didn't fit into the network. I was a fringe dweller and I have remained a fringe dweller all my life.

actually I'm German...

In 1941, during the bombardment of Hong Kong by the Japanese, we sheltered, along with other displaced civilians, in a commandeered school, which served as a medical supply centre for my father.

Immediately after the capitulation we returned to our house, which being mid-level on the peak was intact, having escaped damage from shelling and looting. It was a relief to leave the damaged school and take up residence once more in the familiar surroundings of our own home. Several of the people who had been with us in the school asked if they could come and stay until things had settled. They had no homes to return to, having fled from Kowloon on the other side of the harbour.

Ours was a large house and in addition to my father's assistant, we were soon accommodating a Jewish couple, who years earlier had fled Hitler's Germany, a Portuguese family of six, and the Chinese wife and child of an English soldier. She opted to sleep in the servants' quarters, away from the main house, until she was raped by a Japanese soldier, who justified his deed by thrusting a fistful of military yen into her hand and then walking away.

A few days later about six Japanese officers came and nailed a notice to the front door. Panicking, the Jewish couple made it be known they were actually Germans, and therefore allies, while the Portuguese declared their neutrality.

'What are you going to do about your soldiers?' my mother questioned the officers. 'They came and raped one of our women.'

The officer told us that our house had been commandeered by the army and that we should all move out to somewhere safer as there was to be a victory celebration in a few days time and they couldn't guarantee our safety.

When they left my father vented his suppressed anger on the Jewish and Portuguese families who had so readily aligned themselves with the Japanese. With great restraint, he requested that they leave his house. The Chinese woman and her child moved into the main house with us, until our proposed exodus to Queen Mary's Hospital, where most of the medical staff were quartered.

When the day for our removal came, we all wore Red Cross arm bands to signal our medical affiliations, but even with these we were stopped on our way to the hospital by a sentry at a roadblock who refused to let us pass. There was some parleying, with my father and his assistant trying to think of an alternative route.

'This is the only road we can take,' said my mother, who was very practical. Then she turned and proceeded to shout, in English, at the Japanese sentry. 'Where is your officer?' The situation was bizarre. A Chinese woman speaking English to a Japanese, who clearly did not understand a single word.

Undeterred, my mother continued to communicate, this time in mime, pointing to the soldier's neck. This, he immediately understood, as only the upper ranks had their insignia on their collars. The soldier departed, returning shortly with a fairly high-ranking officer.

'Do you speak English?' my mother questioned him. 'We've got to get to the hospital, do you understand?'

There was no way of knowing if he did but he gestured to us, as if to indicate we could continue. 'Maybe you don't understand this,' said my mother, 'but God bless you!'

'I do understand you,' he replied unexpectedly, in perfect English, 'I was four years in Berlin as a student of theology.'

He sent two soldiers on with us as escorts and we arrived safely at the hospital, where we would stay until we were interned in the prison camp.

Queen Mary's Hospital...

At the hospital, my father put me in charge of the servicing duties for one of the wards. There I made a friend of about the same age, an English youth, Keith Kerr. Keith spoke perfect Japanese, having been brought up in Japan.

We were out roaming together one day when we saw two Chinese with poles across their shoulders, a large pannier balanced at either end, filled with tinned goods.

'What have you got there?' I asked them in Chinese.

'Want to buy some?' one of the men replied.

A Japanese officer appeared, as if from nowhere and began shouting in Japanese. Keith translated. 'He wants to know where they got this food.'

I translated for the Chinese.

'Down the road,' they replied. 'There were open godowns, so we just helped ourselves.' I translated this into English for Keith and he translated it, in turn, into Japanese.

'Tell them they are looters,' the Japanese officer replied, 'and they're going to be shot.' Keith translated for me.

I didn't know what to do. I was unable, at first, to respond at all. In the pause, the Japanese officer had another idea. 'Tell them to pick up a rock.' This was duly translated, but the Chinese mistook his meaning and both selected large rocks to sit down on.

'No,' the Japanese continued. 'No, stand up. Lift it up. Put it above your head.'

The Chinese, becoming more and more afraid, did as they were told. Each time they lowered the heavy weight, the officer flicked them on the nose with his finger.

'What is he going to do to us?' the Chinese asked me. I still couldn't bring myself to tell them what he'd said. We'd already seen incidents where Europeans had been lined up as if for execution, and a Japanese officer had given the command to fire. But instead of machine-gun fire, the soldiers had made mock firing sounds and then collapsed into laughter. Big joke. So I didn't know if this officer was serious in his intentions. He was the only Japanese present and I was tempted to say to the Chinese, 'Look, they're going to shoot you. Run, just run away.' But what if the officer, who had a gun in his holster, decided to use it? What then? Finally, I just told them, 'He's going to take you into town.' This began a lifetime of guilt for me, as I wondered about their fate and whether I should have told them what he had really threatened.

the second-best prison camp in the Far East...

After a few weeks, we were rounded up and taken to Stanley Internment Camp, a compound of living quarters that had been used pre-war to house the wardens in charge of the large prison that stood alongside. This latter was retained as a correction centre by the Japanese. On a nearby hill was a school, St Stephen's College, with attendant bungalows for the teaching staff.

The camp had a mixture of nationalities and each had a section of its own. Two-thirds of the buildings that had once served the white warders were now allocated to married couples and their families. This was called 'Married Quarters'. The other third was given over to American nationals and was called 'American Quarters'. The buildings that used to house the Indian warders now served the European police force, who were deemed to be civilian internees, but the buildings retained the name 'Indian Quarters'. St Stephen's College and its adjoining bungalows housed the overflow from the other quarters and a small contingent of Norwegians. This conglomeration went under several names: 'St Stephen's', 'Bungalows' or 'Norwegian Quarters'.

My four years in the camp were marked by the same good luck that has followed me for most of my life. I was assigned to work in the kitchen, which meant extra food. We were meant to get an extra half-ration for doing our work but it was common knowledge that most people took two and sometimes even three times the usual rations either to eat it themselves or to sell it. The internees knew what was going on so every six months the whole kitchen staff was sacked. For some reason, they kept asking me back, so I was perpetually on one-and-a-half rations, and working in the kitchen gave you extra privileges.

In the camp one was safe in a funny sort of way. There was no anxiety. I had my own 'room' in 'Married Quarters', a little recess under the stairs which I managed to string a curtain across. The rest of the family was lucky enough to get a room to themselves, sleeping on narrow bunks in what used to be the servants' quarters, rather than being crammed in with two or three other families in the overcrowded larger rooms.

It was the second-best prison camp in the Far East. The cushiest was Shanghai. The Japanese looked down upon us because we were civilians but we weren't treated all that badly in comparison to the military camps. We were simply put out in the sticks and left to stagnate.

The camp showed me that people were human. One had been brought up to respect certain values and pay homage to the concept of rank, but in the camp, divisions were blurred. There was an enforced equality but it had Orwellian overtones with some people being more equal than others.

There were so many top-echelon civil servants interned there who behaved badly and people who you'd expect to be difficult, who behaved well. It made me realise that one's position in society had little to do with one's worth. That was the biggest lesson I learnt. You don't judge people. You respond to them for what they are rather than what they represent.

extra rations...

There were a couple of thousand people in the internment camp. The majority of males were either very young or quite mature. Consequently the 200-odd interned police officers carried out the more strenuous duties when they arose. Most of the other young, fit civilians had volunteered for the defence forces. They were armed and uniformed and so after the surrender they were incarcerated with the military in the more notorious prison camps.

I was sixteen when I went in, but at 6′1″, fully grown and quite well-developed because of the extra rations I was getting and all the exercise, carrying sacks of rice and humping things around. I used to come back to my room and find little lumps of sugar on my bed and once there was a scarf with my initials on it—gifts from unknown admirers who later came forward to make themselves known.

There was an attractive woman at the camp whom we used to call Mata Hari. Her husband was an officer interned in the military camp. In our spare time we had dances on the flat roof of one of the buildings, with somebody's gramophone blaring out, and it was at one of these, when I was dancing with her, that she whipped me behind one of the chimney pots and started to make love to me.

About the same time I was introduced by John Sloss, a friend I had made at the camp, to a girl more my own age and my affections were immediately transferred. Her name was Penny and John had known her in pre-camp days.

John Sloss became the most influential person in my life at this time, also introducing me to the works of authors like Aldous Huxley and George Orwell, whom I would not normally have been interested in.

Penny was a virgin, though not strictly *intacta*. She had been deflowered by a fountain pen, wielded by one of her dormitory chums when she attended Rodean. We became lovers and I found that the demands of Mata Hari were interfering with my new relationship.

John was still a virgin and was always questioning me about my love life, so I devised a way of settling my dilemma. I introduced him to Mata Hari.

not even friends...

Besides using the flat roofs for dancing, other social activities were indulged in. This became obvious to the Japanese in charge, whose own residence was on a hill overlooking the roofs.

A notice was published by the authorities and posted on the camp notice board for all to read.

> IT HAS COME TO OUR ATTENTION THAT THE ROOFS ARE BEING USED FOR IMMORAL PURPOSES. THE AUTHORITIES DO NOT MIND MARRIED OR ENGAGED COUPLES USING THESE FACILITIES, BUT WE HAVE BEEN INFORMED THAT SOME OF THE PEOPLE ARE NOT EVEN FRIENDS.

Penny and I used the roofs but sheltered under a blanket canopy until one night we were confronted by an irate Korean guard brandishing his rifle with a fixed bayonet. He had evidently been ordered to find out what was going on under the concealing shelter.

Shouting and swishing his rifle (the Japanese and the Koreans always seemed to shout their requests) he urged us to quit our nest and we scurried *down* a ladder this time—the second expulsion from Eden.

From then onwards we resorted to my cubbyhole under the stairs, which though prone to interruptions from passers-by, was a jolly sight less harrowing.

honour, not food...

It was the police lads who used to pilfer oil from a sump in the godowns, originally the storehouses for the British troops, which the Japanese had now taken over. My friends, Brendan and Clifton, decided we should try it too, disregarding the fact that I worked in the kitchen and had no need of extra oil for cooking. It was a case of honour rather than food because if the Japanese had caught us, we would have been in trouble.

We got over the barbed wire, risked getting shot and made our way to the godowns, only to find that the sump was bone dry. The police lads had done their job only too well.

All the provisions that had been stored in the godowns had been cleared out some time earlier, with the Japanese using people from the camp to transfer it to lorries. Naturally, everyone was pocketing what they could and I remember putting a small tin of butter between my legs, so that it rested in the crotch of my trousers, a ruse I was to use again many years later.

The Japanese knew what we were up to and lined us all up to be searched. I stood there petrified but they passed me by. Next to me was an American priest, calmly standing there, dressed in his cassock. The Japanese soldier began to pat his body. One tin . . . two tins. More patting. Six tins were finally withdrawn. Everyone was laughing by now, even the soldier, who moved off to the next person.

'Hey!' the priest called. The soldier turned to look at him. 'You may as well have this one too!' and he fished out one last tin from the voluminous cassock. There was a lot of humour in the camp and a lot of education too, but for me, the priority was food for my belly. Food for thought took second place.

in the cemetery...

On days when we were allowed to go swimming at the nearby beach, we were accompanied by a Korean guard, the Japanese troops being too precious to be used as guards for civilians. At first, Indian members of the Hong Kong Police Force were used but they either fraternised with their former European colleagues and superiors, or settled previous scores in a none too gentle manner.

So it was a Korean guard who ambled alongside those wishing to swim and kept an eye on them in case they tried to escape or hustled them back to the camp if there was an air raid, or if the road was to be cleared for VIP Japanese military transport.

Whistles were blown to announce either of these events and on one such occasion, a friend, Glascott Dawson-Groves, and I found ourselves deafened by whistles and inadvertently witnessed the prison gates open, before we were herded back to camp. Out roared a Black Maria and several open limousines, filled with Japanese officers. Soldiers were perched on the running boards blowing whistles, shouting and waving to us to get out of the way. The entourage narrowly missed us, and as the Black Maria passed we saw some European faces pressed against the bars of the back window of the van.

'They're going to shoot us!' a voice cried out. I recognised one of the faces as a fellow internee who had been arrested a couple of weeks before, along with some others. The Japanese had been informed that they were hiding a wireless in the camp and I had seen them digging up a wrapped object, supervised by the Japanese. When the covering was torn off, it revealed the contraband item. They were immediately taken away and nothing more had been heard of them in spite of enquiries by our own camp committee.

Now here they were, being carted away in a Black Maria. We knew from previous experience that if the van turned to the right, they were being taken to town. If it turned to the left, its destination was the field we knew was used for executions. It turned left.

We sprinted off and from a vantage point on the cemetery which overlooked the field, we saw the Japanese herding the men out of the truck, about twenty in all. A long trench had been dug to one side and the men, Chinese, Indians and four Europeans, were made to kneel beside it. The Japanese shot them in the back of the head and just pushed them in.

We were scared stiff because we had seen it, and as we thought that the four men must have been those from our camp, we informed our camp committee. They immediately demanded more information from the Japanese, making us even more scared in case the Japanese wanted to grill us.

It had such a traumatic effect on us that Glascott and I never brought up the subject again, in all the time we were in the camp.

the painted word...

During my enforced detention I developed an aversion to the maltreatment of books. In the camp there was a small library of books, which because of the situation, became all the more precious. They were mass-produced pulpy editions of Agatha Christie, Rider Haggard, Baroness Orczy and the like.

For some time my twin ambitions were to be an actor, because one got to kiss all the pretty girls, or a painter, because of the bohemian lifestyle, and of course, the fact that artists had the chance to paint ladies in the nude. So I swapped my ration of cigarettes for a small box of watercolour paints, but what to do for paper?

The liberators take us for a victory lap around the camp.

The camp notice board.

The flyleaves of the library books seemed to be the obvious solution, and I wasn't the only desecrator. Soon, the books consisted only of covers and the abrupt beginning of the printed word. No turning over of virginal pages, invitingly spread for artistic violation.

All went well until one day I showed my paintings—records of the camp's events—to a young lady whom I wanted to impress, forgetting in my desire for praise that she was one of the people who helped to run the library. She took one look at the paintings, my first records without a camera, and gave her opinion. It had nothing to do with the images. 'You're the culprit!' she howled. 'And to think I even helped you to choose which books to borrow.'

Humiliation! I have been trying to make up for my transgression ever since, determined to respect the form of the book, no matter what its content.

yes sir, no sir...

My whole life was affected by what happened in the prison camp. I was sixteen when I was thrown in, the age when you start to think about things and where discipline comes into your life. It is the age when you start to consider other people, who they are and what you think of them.

When the camp finished I knew I couldn't stay in Hong Kong. It would have meant working under people I'd just spent four years with, people who'd behaved badly. They were the people I would have to go to for a job, the people I would have to respect.

There were certain things which the camp ingrained deeply within me, things that are no longer valid. I get angry when I see food wasted, even though we're not starving, even though it's not going to save the world. But when you've been through this period, this phase of being in need of food, you hate to see the waste. To this day if I see food left on a plate, I have to eat it.

Flight Mechanic Morley in action.

grey suits me best…

When the war was over, we were repatriated to England and the question arose as to whether I was obliged to do national service, having just spent four years in an internment camp.

The Citizens' Advice Bureau advised me, wrongly as it finally turned out, that as it had been a civilian camp, it would make no difference. If I volunteered, however, I could choose which branch of the services I entered. I chose the RAF because grey suited me best.

I was assigned to be a Flight Mechanic Engineer and had to undergo all the necessary training. I got through the theory well enough, but I hated the practical side, so after a period of being a complete failure as a mechanic, I managed to get transferred to Station Headquarters and clerical duties.

When I got to England I had no status at all. I was on my own. I was classless, but I wasn't a real everyman. I had my prejudices. Curiously, it was the same in the RAF as it had been in the camp. I was exposed to the type of people who could benefit me, people who come from influential families and who later became instrumental in my work as a photographer.

Coincidence, which played such an important part in my life, once more took matters into its own hands.

After my initial training in the North of England I was posted to, of all places, Brize Norton, just a few miles from Oxford where John Sloss was now an undergraduate, living out of college in his family house. His father had returned to Hong Kong to resume his position at the university there.

John had the whole house to himself, and a housekeeper to do all the chores. A lot of parties took place at the weekends, which more often than not found me in residence with the occasional WAAF whom I had brought along for company.

Halfway through my two years service I met a chap called Ken Cootes-Smith, who was a painter, and with him I used to discuss art. He suggested I go to evening classes in Oxford and later that I should apply for a grant to go to art school.

The education officer in the RAF—another double-barrelled name which eludes me—gave me the nod and suggested I go to see Coulson-Davies at Twickenham Art School, and to mention his name.

When I saw Coulson-Davies, he told me that I would have to go before a tribunal of artists and government inspectors, and show my work. If I was awarded a grant, there was a place for me at Twickenham.

In order to obtain the grant it was necessary to hang up one's work in a large area in an educational institution, full of other applicants' work. All I had to show were the little drawings I had done on the torn flyleaves of books in the camp. The rest of the hall was filled with fantastic pieces of art, commercial art, paintings and the like as half of the applicants had been at art school when the war had started. They were now intending to pick up where they had left off. In the midst of it all were my grotty little drawings of Japanese soldiers and camp life, making it quite humiliating for me.

As well as the display there were the interviews with the panel of artists and government inspectors. 'We've seen your work Mr Morley. Now if you do get a grant, you realise that you would have to do the commercial art course, because we are not giving out any more fine art places.'

I really wanted to go to art school and become a painter but I accepted their conditions readily enough. In the waiting room outside, the concierge unexpectedly came up to me. 'Don't worry mate,' he said confidentially. 'You're in!' Wink, wink. 'You've got it!'

'How do you know?' I asked. He shrugged. A couple of weeks later I received notice that I'd been accepted, on a scholarship of £208 a year. I feel certain that I had got my grant because of the subject matter of my drawings, rather than any artistic merit. 'Poor sod!' I could hear them saying. 'He's had a rough time. Give him a grant.'

pseudo-Picasso...

I was at Twickenham Art School for three years, studying commercial art. There was an intellectual division between the fine artists and the commercial artists, the latter being merely a profession, as opposed to a calling.

My painting influences were artists like Utrillo and Braque, because one could imitate one of their pictures without really being able to draw too well. One could be a pseudo-Picasso, and along with a certain naivety, I could put down an effect.

One of my teachers was an Australian, F.W. Wentworth-Sheilds, whose father had been Bishop of New South Wales. At 24, I was one of the oldest students and there was some jealousy about the fact that I was always discussing things with Sheilds.

'Well Morley, why don't you have the day off?' Sheilds would tell me. 'Go to the Victoria and Albert. Have a look around.' Or:

'Why don't you do a painting Morley?'

'What of?'

'Whatever you like.'

So I would do a painting, in the John Piper style, with black skies, and one of the other students, called Sparks, would question me, 'Why are you painting?'

'Sheilds suggested I could.'

So Sparks, who was a rather swaggering young chap, went up to Sheilds:

'Here Mr Sheilds, Morley's painting?'

'Yes Sparks.'

'Can I paint?'

'I don't know, can you?'

'No, I mean, can I do a painting?'

'No. You've got other work to do, haven't you?'

'Why can Morley paint and I can't?'

'Simply because Morley is Morley and Sparks is Sparks.'

It put me in a funny position. I was granted all these privileges but only with this particular teacher. Perhaps we saw eye to eye because I didn't take everything all that seriously and it appealed to his Australian sense of humour, which set him apart from the more stuffy members of the teaching fraternity. With some of the latter, particularly the fine art teachers, I was often in competition, but not over paintings.

My age and physical stature were in some ways a challenge to them and perhaps they felt threatened by me. The situation could be summed up by an incident in the life-drawing class one day. We had a model, Joan, who was an ex-student. Half the kids and all of the teachers knew her. Now here she was modelling in the nude and suddenly a couple of teachers, who'd never appeared in life-drawing before, started coming to classes.

'Freddie![1]' Joan called out one day, at the end of class.

'What?' I replied, still clearing away my things.

'Turn around.'

As I turned, she jumped into my arms, at the same moment as one of the painting masters opened the door. He looked at me with hatred and without a word, turned on his heels and walked out. Nothing was said to me but some of the others in the class were hauled over the coals about the incident.

I wasn't really a good student but managed to get various diplomas in commercial art, ending with a First Class and a Distinction. But these were only the internal classifications. I never tackled the National Design Diploma, which the more serious students did.

Sheilds continued his patronage by helping me to get my first job at the advertising agency, Colman, Prentis & Varley.

let fate do it for me...

I never thought about what was happening in my life, of how I kept landing on my feet. I didn't expect things to

1. I was known as Freddie to friends and family to avoid confusion with my father, Lewis John.

happen and I'm too superstitious to go out of my way to make them happen. That would be tempting the gods. I let fate do it for me.

So fate took a hand when I was working at my second advertising agency after art school. It was a few storeys up and I happened to be looking out the window one day when I saw two girls passing by down in the street. Curiously, they looked up and one was a girl I knew, Janet, John Sloss' girlfriend and later, his wife. I sprinted down to talk to them and they told me they were only in London for a short time as they were now living in Paris.

'You've always wanted to be an artist, Freddie, and live in Paris,' said Janet. 'We've got a big studio, come and stay with us.'

I sprinted back upstairs to the Agency. 'I quit!' I told them.

'What do you mean, you quit?' they responded.

'I quit, I'm going to live in Paris.'

Montparnasse...

There were three American girls living in the studio in Paris: Janet, Jody and Brookie. They were all working and didn't want me to contribute financially to the food, so I did all the shopping and cooking. It was fun at first, with me living in the big studio with the grand piano and each of them in their own rooms on an upper, split-level. Then Jody fell in love with a French diplomat and I was chosen as the father confessor.

'Fred,' she told me, 'Yves wants to go to bed with me. What should I do?' I advised her to follow her instincts in the matter.

'I've done everything,' she continued, '. . . everything except *that*, and when I do it, I want to do it with a 100 per cent American boy.'

It got to the point where I had to move to one of the outer studios, with a tin roof, to avoid her confidences.

Three young American women, living unprotected in Paris at the beginning of the 1950s. It was an unnerving prospect to conjure with, particularly for their mothers, and one day a large woman knocked at the door. 'You must be Fred,' she greeted me. 'When Brookie wrote home and said she was living with an artist, I thought I'd better fly over and look for myself. Now that I've met you, I know everything's OK. Call me Ma!'

Although my relationship with Brookie was purely platonic, I didn't know whether to be flattered or offended, but 'Ma' did buy some of my paintings, as did some of the other rich Americans living in Paris.

Schiaparelli's 'Shocking'...

I was four months in Paris, painting and attending some art classes at the Académie La Grande Chaumière. Then I started to get homesick. At art school, one of the students I'd met was Patricia Clifford, who was now working as a commercial artist in London. After these months away, the resolution formed of returning to London and asking Pat to marry me.

I remember walking down the Rue du Faubourg St-Honoré when literally, a flash caught my eye from the window of one of the jewellery shops. In the display was a little Georgian ring with five flat stones, looking like lumps of lead... Georgian diamonds. I pulled out the money and bought it on the spot but later became panic-stricken that I might have to pay duty on it.

As well, I bought a bottle of Schiaparelli's 'Shocking' which at that time came in the shape of a clothing mannequin with a glass dome on top—a beautiful little thing. The problem of getting both gifts back to England, without paying any extra money which I did not now have, became uppermost in my mind.

This was my 'Paris, plaster of Paris' phase when I was painting directly onto plaster of Paris which had been poured into a support. The plaster soaked up the watercolour or poster paint, or whatever I was using and then I would varnish it to bring the colours back. The finished works were very heavy and not very strong. One subject was a white dove, so I conceived the idea of drilling a hole in the beak and inserting the Georgian ring into it, as if it were part of the picture. Now, I could legitimately identify it as part of a work of art if the need arose.

I went by boat-train back to England, knowing that I would have to go through customs at Dover. About six of my plaster pictures were packed together, on top of my rucksack, in which was concealed the beautiful pink box that held Schiaparelli's 'Shocking'.

It was on the boat that I began to worry again, so I went down to the lavatories, discarded the pink box and put the little mannequin, with its glass dome, into the crotch of my trousers.

The moment came and I walked through customs in my dufflecoat, staggering under the weight of the paintings on my back.

'Anything to declare?' came the inevitable question.

'Nope,' I said, trembling like mad under the bravura. But I made it through and was on my way to the train when . . . craackk . . . then clink, clink, clink . . . and glass was spilling out of the bottom of my trousers.

In the lavatory on the train I investigated the damage. The bottle was still all right and it was the glass dome I had somehow smashed.

With having to resort to these elaborate precautions to prevent disaster continually cropping up in my life, it's easy to see how I suffered from ulcers, the photographer's chronic disease, long before I became a photographer.

other interests . . .

When I got back to England, I got in touch with Pat and arranged to meet her at a little pub in Twickenham. We were sitting down with our drinks when I handed over the ring.

'What's this?' she asked.

'An engagement ring,' I replied.

'Are you asking me to marry you?'

'Yeah!'

We were married and knowing that I could not exist as an out-of-work painter, I got a job as a telephone operator, which meant I could work at night, leaving my days free for my other interests.

In Paris I had taken reportage-style photographs in the Cartier Bresson mould and back in England, although most of my day was devoted to painting, I still dabbled in photography. I used to show these to a friend I'd made, Herbert Freudenheim, a scientific photographer who did silk-screen work in the basement of one of the advertising agencies I'd worked in. He liked my work and advised me to take it to Norman Hall who had a magazine devoted to photography and who had started the new English photographic school.

Hall was non-committal but asked to keep the work and eventually told me to write a few words about myself, with the result that I had a six-page spread in the magazine. I was designated a new 'Young Briton Discovery'.

In the same year, 1957, my son, Lewis Patrick, was born and the following year I had my first published photograph in *The Tatler*, the beginning of a long association with the magazine. It took a further year to give me the confidence that I could in fact earn enough money to support us as a photographer. I then gave up my job as a telephone operator and started to work as a freelance photographer from my home.

It was 1959, the end of an old decade and also the end of an era in many respects. We were hovering on the edge of the sixties, unaware of the revolution that was about to take place.

THE SIXTIES

There were lines of connection that started in my personal life with friends I had known in Hong Kong and in the camp and these branched out into the worlds of high society, through *The Tatler* and showbiz, through my theatre connections.

No matter what I thought of my subjects, whether I liked them or thought they were pretentious, I was hypocritical enough to be nice, and vulnerable enough to want to be liked, and pretentious enough myself to enjoy hobnobbing occasionally with a marchioness.

Also I was there for a purpose, to take photographs. I did not touch my cap to people because they happened to have a title. The camp had taught me that much. I simply treated people on a one-to-one basis, taking my cue from how they treated me.

In the sixties there was a breaking-down of class barriers but there was never real equality. Rather it was a form of inverted snobbery where it became quite fashionable to have a working-class 'mate' and be accepted. I think it was a turning point where a lot of sacred cows were being sacrificed: the sanctity of 'our beloved institutions' that had been put in place during the Victorian era was being questioned. The sixties saw not so much a liberation as a breaking-down of discipline, and the removal of restrictions on what could be said and could be made public. Theatre, with which I was about to become involved, was very much a part of it.

Technically I was never trained as a photographer and I never really took it seriously, as I did, for instance, with painting. So there is a sense in which I feel that I never really created my photographs. A lot of it was luck.

the wrong place at the wrong time...

An awful lot of my success came from being in the right place at the right time and from my taking advantage of a situation that presented itself without any initial instigation on my part.

There were overseas assignments from many different sources: fashion, advertising, travel and public relations. Plum opportunities constantly fell in my lap, commissions to photograph people still in the embryonic state of their future notoriety. I had very little of that hard graft and rejection that so many others in the profession had to endure before . . . that awful term . . . 'making it'. I worked hard when the opportunity presented itself but I seldom worked hard to achieve the opportunity.

I cannot help feeling that this concept of 'the right place at the right time' is a form of hindsight, however. I have thousands of negatives of people who thought they were in the right place at the right time. Talented people with all the ingredients for success, but they did not make it, so now one must assume they were in the wrong place at the wrong time, if the theory is to hold water.

I am constantly aware of my luck at being in the so-called right place at the right time, but at the same time, constantly nagged by the fear that my good fortune will be abruptly terminated. When you are not wholly responsible for your laurels there is always an element of not being fully confident, of not being in control. It's like sitting in the pilot's seat of a Boeing which is on automatic pilot, equipped with a faulty switch and knowing that you just got your wings by flying a Gypsy Moth.

I feel in many ways I was just clicking the shutter. The fact that I clicked it at the right time means that these images now exist. I was a sloppy photographer, my only achievement being perhaps that I had an attitude that was different to someone else, and so my pictures are different.

The Tatler and Bystander...

The Tatler and Bystander, to give it its full title, was the magazine to be seen in. If you were not fortunate enough to achieve that honour, at least you could be seen carrying it around.

Janet, John Sloss, self, Shura Shihwarg, and Denise.

My first published photograph for *The Tatler*, in November 1958, was also one of my first published 'commercial' jobs, and for this I have Shura Shihwarg to thank.

My association with Shura had begun when John Sloss introduced us. John's father was Vice-Chancellor of Hong Kong University where Shura had been studying. His family were White Russians, political refugees from the 1917 Revolution, now living in China.

With the outbreak of hostilities in Hong Kong, Shura had joined the local volunteer defence force and was interned with the military after the colony's surrender to the victorious Japanese. John and myself, who were too young for military service, were interned in a civilian camp.

After the war Shura met up with John's father and asked for help in getting to the United Kingdom, rather than being repatriated, to his parents, back in China. This was successful and he got a place at Oxford and a grant to support him while he studied. At Oxford, he was enrolled at Wadham, where a certain Lindsay Anderson was also in attendance.

Now Shura was living in London, trying to work as a freelance journalist but the ultimate scoop was always too evasive, always out of reach.

He had seen a recent photograph of mine and decided that it was a commercial proposition because its subject was a young playwright, Kenneth Jupp, who had just won the best play of the year award. I had taken Jupp to a series of different locations, one of which was the Albert Memorial, a heavy slab of marble and other exotic stones, sculpted into a frieze of males, females and famous literary and historical figures. The lesser mortals represented 'The Empire' on which the sun never set, and they wound in a never-ending procession around the centrepiece, the prince for whom the memorial was named, who sat aloft, on an ornate throne, under a Gothic canopy.

On the day in question, the immobile prince seemed grateful for his shelter. The sun, which never sets, had temporarily disappeared and it was pouring with rain. I decided that the newly honoured bard should be photographed alongside his marble peers and that it would add a certain piquancy if he were to walk in the rain with his umbrella up. This he agreed to and I ran alongside, snapping away in the pouring torrent.

The dailies had already printed Jupp's story so Shura decided that a weekly magazine would be the obvious outlet. Because of its rather up-market connotations, he decided on *The Tatler*.

The photograph was duly pubished and the editor was impressed enough to phone me and suggest I do some more work for them.

One of the first jobs was an article which I also wrote, because of a misunderstanding. Over the telephone, the editor was explaining that he wanted me to photograph a series of shop owners for an article called, 'Shop-Keepers Supreme'—people like Sir Richard Burbridge of Harrod's, Dr Leonard Simpson of Simpson's and Sir Simon Marks of Marks and Spencer's. He was reeling off these names so fast that I was at a loss to remember who was who and I asked him to repeat them.

'Can you write?' he demanded.

'Yes,' I said, grabbing a pen to write down the list.

'Very well, you write it, I'll send you the details,' and he hung up.

He had assumed by my 'yes' that I was a writer and so had allocated me the copy as well. I didn't have the nerve to ring back and tell him of the misunderstanding. It was my first feature and I didn't want to lose it, so when the list and arrangements arrived in the post, I set out with camera and notebook.

When published, the article included a full-page photograph among other smaller images. The byline was in large capital letters: 'PHOTOGRAPHIC REPORTING BY LEWIS MORLEY'. I had become a journalist by default.

I did more photo-journalism for *The Tatler*, including the very un-*Tatler* subject of fun fairs at Hampstead Heath. As I became more involved with other work, I found writing too time-consuming and in later articles I worked with bona fide writers, a better arrangement for all concerned.

Some years later when I had become established as a photographer, I bumped into the editor of *The Tatler*, while travelling on the underground.

'I see you've given up writing altogether to become a full-time photographer,' he commented.

'I've always been a photographer,' I replied. 'I only wrote because I didn't have the nerve to tell you otherwise on that first feature you gave me.'

'I always thought you were a writer who took photographs,' he said, laughing, 'not the other way around!'

faint heart ne'er won fair lady...

My work as a freelance photographer, working from home, continued to grow, until it became obvious I could leave my job at the Telephone Exchange and take up photography full-time. The shared bathroom at our digs, which served as my darkroom, was far from ideal, often punctuated by hammerings on the door as some impatient co-lodger demanded his rights to the bath, currently occupied by my floating prints.

Shura introduced me to the photographer, Alex Sterling, and I began working from his studio in the 'Pheasantry', a complex of buildings which housed a club as well as several other studios. It was not a happy time as Alex did not share any of my attitudes to photography.

The people at *The Tatler* knew I was unhappy with the arrangements and it was they who sent me to No 6 Marshall Street, Soho, a small, narrow street without any redeeming features. The building was soot-stained red-brick, as was the building a few hundred yards away, displaying the blue and white plaque which detailed that William Blake had once lived there. I am certain that no such plaque will ever adorn No 6 Marshall Street, to herald the fact that Lewis Morley had once worked there at Panaramic [sic] Studios.

As I climbed the narrow stairs to the top floor for my appointment, I was wondering how on earth *The Tatler* could send me to a place like this. Panaramic Studios were also contributors to the magazine and they apparently had space in their set-up for another photographer.

The stairs led past an area humming with the sound of sewing machines, the people scurrying back and forth with their arms loaded with clothing and knitwear—a ragtrade sweatshop. Their offices, I discovered, were on the floor above.

As I walked past the open door, I heard an inner door being hurriedly opened and turned to see a short, rotund, very ethnic gentleman peering at me through thick, horn-rimmed glasses. His face registered disappointment and abruptly he disappeared, slamming the door behind him.

Reaching the top floor, I knocked on the door of Panaramic Studios and was greeted by another rotund gentleman, also wearing horn-rimmed glasses, but this one was frightfully English. He introduced himself as Jonathon and led me through a minute studio to an even smaller office where I met the owner, William Donaldson.

I was taken out to a slap-up lunch and negotiations were made for me to start as soon as possible. Over lunch I became aware of the reason for the 'awfully nice' tag that *The Tatler* had bestowed upon the studio. Four of the five directors were ex-public school and Varsity. I became part of Panaramic Studios the following Monday.

The smallness of the studio didn't really affect me as most of my assignments consisted of location work but the other photographer made full use of it, as still-life and the odd fashion house shot were his main occupation. Once in residence it wasn't too long before the reason for the downstairs ethnic gentleman's behaviour became obvious.

We had the usual stream of models doing their rounds of the studios with their portfolios, and the wooden stairs resounded with the click of their heels as they trod their way up to us on the top floor. This sound was a signal for Mr L. as we shall call him, to open his office door to see what was passing.

No sooner had a model arrived for her booking or sat down in the reception to show her photographs, than the phone would ring and Mr L. would be pleading for the girl to call into his office on the way down, to try on some new imports that had arrived. Although this was a fairly regular routine, I tried to discourage Mr L. from the practice, telling him that if he needed his sweaters modelled, he would have to book a model and pay her the regular fee. The minimum booking was one hour and Mr L. argued that it was impractical for him to book a model for an assignment that might take only one or two minutes. Anyway, he reasoned, he always gave the girls a choice of sweater, or a dress which would cost more than the fee for a two-hour booking.

His custom was to vacate his office, in which the girls changed, chaperoned by his secretary and I had no real objections until one day, returning from an assignment, I happened to be passing his office at the appropriate time. Mr L. was standing outside his closed office door, looking through the hammered glass panel at the bubbly, undulating image of a girl disrobing.

From then on I hung up with a curt 'No' whenever he telephoned with his familiar request but then came the day when I was going downstairs with Milly, a willowy blonde model whom I used quite often. Our path was blocked by chubby Mr L.

'Please' he pleaded. 'I have just received a consignment of lovely sweaters. Please,' he begged Milly, 'just try one on for me?'

I told him there was a taxi downstairs waiting for us, and we were running late. 'I have it ready, here,' he said, clutching a white cable-knit sweater.

'OK,' relented Milly, feeling sorry for him, and because we were pressed for time, she didn't bother going into the office but whipped off the sweater she was wearing, there and then.

Milly was tall, with very small, firm breasts and she never wore a bra. Mr L. was short, so short that her breasts were in a direct line with, and about twelve inches from his goggling eyes. She held out her arms to take the garment which slipped from Mr L.'s trembling ones, his clutch transferring from the sweater to his chest. He gulped, unable to breathe. Milly bent down, picked it up and put it on.

'OK?' she asked.

He nodded dumbly, his whole body shaking in time with his head. Milly took the sweater off, pushed it into his nerveless hands and slipped her own sweater back on. 'See ya,' she said. 'Come on Lewis,' and she grabbed my hand and hurried down the stairs to the waiting cab.

The next morning as I was on my way up to the studio, I was stopped by Mr L.'s secretary. Mr L. was not going to be in this morning, she informed me. He had suffered a heart attack soon after yesterday's incident.

He was away from work for about a week. When he returned, he never phoned up again.

gone, and never called me mother…

There is a complicated story behind the creation of Lewis Morley Studios which occurred about one year after I had joined Panaramic. A purge there eliminated all the personnel, except Martin the assistant and Willy Donaldson, the managing director, who became co-owner with me in the new business.

We decided a secretary was essential for the smooth running of the studio, so along came Miss Hounslow. 'Take a letter Miss Jones' conjured up the established, but in my experience, false vision of a smart young thing in a tight skirt, who crossed her legs to reveal a little too much of her nylons and who sat with pencil poised above the open pad, ready for dictation or action.

Miss Hounslow, taking a letter or any other related action raised none of these images, not even when one's imagination was pushed to the outer limits. She was in her mid-thirties, a plump, proper creature with horn-rimmed spectacles and a very calming personality. With the fantasy of Miss Jones embedded firmly in my mind, I was at first, unenthusiastic, but Miss Hounslow didn't push her qualifications, which were more than adequate, or sell her efficiency, which was obvious. 'This place has a nice atmosphere,' she said. 'I've never worked with a photographer before. I find the idea a little frightening and a little exciting because I don't know what to expect.'

She seduced me with her lack of guile and her candid replies to my questions and she started the following Monday.

There was one idiosyncrasy I couldn't stop. The formality of calling me 'Sir'. I tried on many occasions to get her to call me Lewis, but no, Willy was Mr Donaldson and I was 'Sir' although occasionally she would relax and call me 'Mr Morley'. Martin, the assistant, was addressed as Martin, or if he ever caused her displeasure, 'Young man!' in a reprimanding tone. So naturally she was 'Miss Hounslow' to all of us.

From the beginning she was a gem. The invoices went out on time, she answered the phone without fluster and gave the impression that everything was under control, which it was. Coffee was always there when wanted and although she was, like most of us in the sixties, a heavy smoker, you never caught her with a lit cigarette when a client was around.

This state of celibate bliss between the studio and Miss Hounslow was shattered one morning when sex reared its ugly head. On that fateful morning, her quiet demeanour was replaced by an almost catatonic trance.

'Good morning Mr Morley,' she mumbled, nursing an unlit cigarette which was shaking like a conductor's baton. I flicked my lighter into life and held it out to her. Her first puff was followed by a cough and a flood of tears. Between sobs I managed to hear: 'I don't want to, but I have to . . .' I hurriedly boiled some water in the electric kettle to make her a cup of calming tea.

She stubbed out her cigarette and took a few short sips of tea to regain her composure, but her eyes once more welled with tears. 'I'm getting married,' she managed to choke out, the dam breaking.

'Miss Hounslow,' I chided, giving her my handkerchief. 'You should be happy, not crying.' But the awful thought occurred to me: *has our Miss Hounslow got herself pregnant?* Miss Hounslow 'in the club' was almost unimaginable. She had never even mentioned a boyfriend. I tried to make her more tea but she took control.

'That's my job, Sir' she said, and between sips and dabbing at her eyes, the whole surprising revelation emerged. Miss Hounslow had been walking out, as the saying goes, with an American serviceman, stationed in England. His tour of duty completed, he wanted to return to the United States, taking our Miss Hounslow with him as his wife.

We missed Miss Hounslow, who left, smiling through her tears. Then one afternoon the telephone rang. 'Mr Morley?' said a familiar voice. 'It's Miss Hounslow. I'm at the airport. We're taking off soon and I wanted to ring you to say goodbye, and to thank you for everything.' There was a long pause. 'Can I ask you a favour?' she continued presently.

'Yes,' I replied.

'Can I call you by your first name please?'

'Of course you can,' I answered, feeling very touched.

'Thank you Sir,' she said, and hung up.

I felt like a bit player in a Victorian melodrama. 'Gone! . . . and never called me mother!'

And I still don't know *her* first name.

concerning spontaneity . . .

Despite all the taboos being broken, things were not really all that liberated at that point in the early sixties. Contraceptives were problematic, unmarried mothers were still very much stigmatised, and marriage seemed inevitable for many. The pill had not yet taken hold and French letters signified a too calculated approach to the supposedly spontaneous encounter. Coitus interruptus was more the norm and many of the double standards were still firmly in place.

For a single girl to get the pill she would have to visit the family doctor and conceal the offending article from the prying eyes of her parents at home. There was also the notion that a girl on the pill was taking things too much into her own hands—anticipating sexual encounters with an unmaidenly directness. So when the inevitable happened and women became pregnant, they generally married if they were working-class, or considered an abortion if they were middle-class and could afford it.

the strains of Mersey are not always quality . . .

Women's Own wanted some photographs of Brian Epstein for an article written by one of their journalists. Epstein was hot news. He was the manager of the Beatles, the once obscure Liverpudlian pop group that he had, in the beginning, no intention of managing. The 'Fab Four' phenomenon had assumed the nightmare proportions of a Topsy out of control. It grew and grew and grew.

I travelled to Liverpool for the assignment where a room had been reserved for me at the Adelphi Hotel. A message was waiting at the reception desk. 'Mr Epstein will see you at 11 a.m. A car will be sent to pick you up.'

At eleven o'clock I was waiting as arranged and precisely on the hour a young man rushed into the foyer, saw me standing with my gear and strode over. 'Hello. You must be Mr Morley. I'm Brian Epstein.' I didn't have to be told. His face was already familiar but I was surprised that he had called in person.

As the chauffeur was gently easing the Rolls Royce out of the hotel grounds, Epstein turned to me and said, 'Well, where do you want to start?' I suggested we visit the places mentioned in the interview.

'Are you familiar with Liverpool?' he asked.

Fade back a decade or more to when I was serving in the RAF and had to travel to Liverpool to say goodbye to my parents who were travelling overseas. We were stationed nearby so I applied for an afternoon off to bid them fond farewell, and was granted a 72-hour pass! Three days! 'What a skive!' said my mates. I'd been overjoyed at the RAF's generosity but the idea of spending three days in Liverpool after a brief meeting and parting was most depressing. It was the late forties, long before the musical revolution and there wasn't much to detain, or entertain me there.

After the last notes of 'Auld Lang Syne' had faded and the hooting of the tugs and the ship's horn had subsided, my depression was heightened by the sight of the ship forcing its way through the thick fog. It was completely enveloped in a matter of minutes. Compared with any other town the quality of Mersey was pretty well strained and certainly could not compete with the bright lights of London, only a few hours away by train. The remainder of my leave was spent at the Nuffield Centre, smack in the middle of London's

New York.

Somerset Maugham.

Osbert Sitwell.

Barry Humphries at The Establishment.

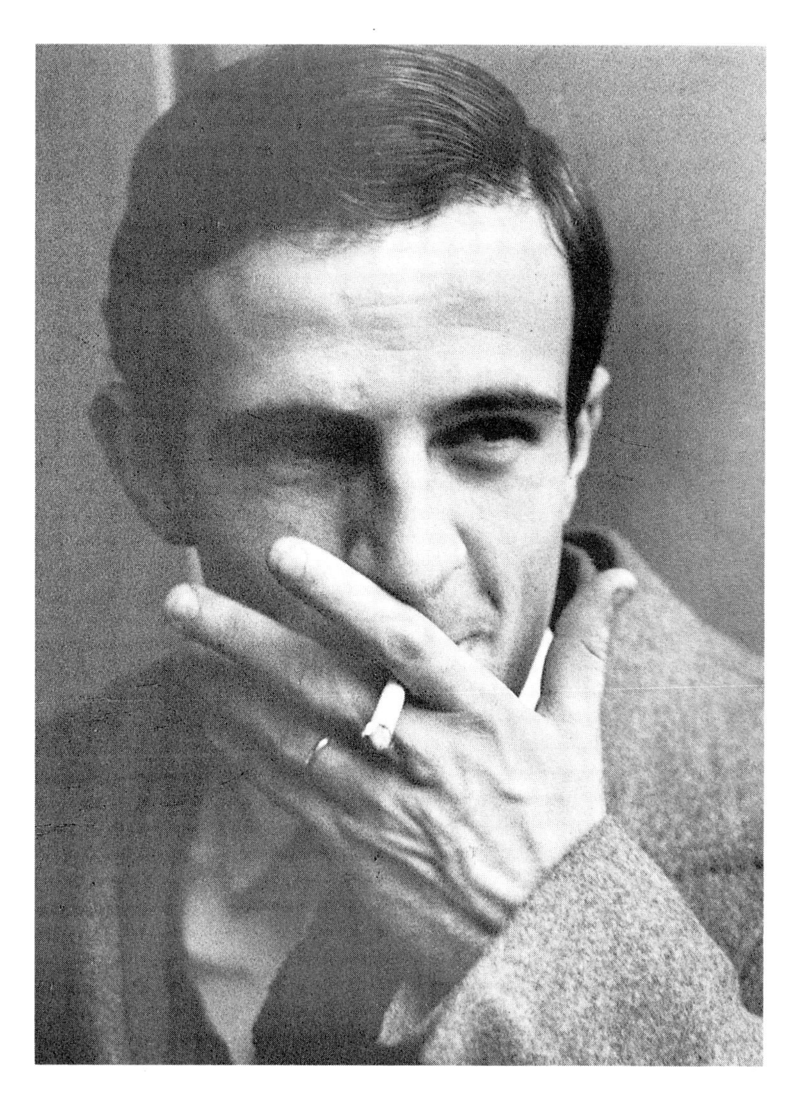

Francois Truffaut.

Jean Shrimpton.

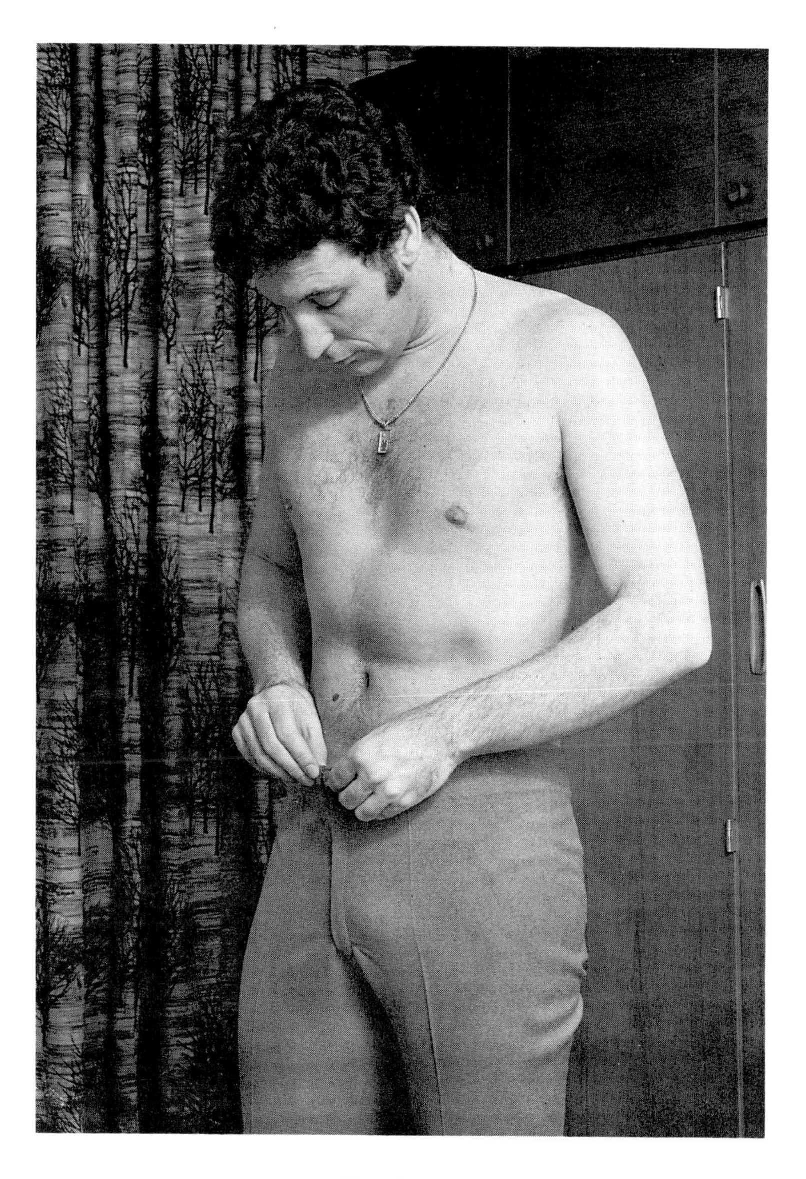

Tom Jones.

Catherine Deneuve with David Bailey.

Justin de Villeneuve with Twiggy.

Peter O'Toole.

Brian Epstein.

Salvador Dali.

Cecil Beaton.

John Betjeman.

Count Robert de Vogue.

Joe Orton.

West End. It was a servicemen's club where the food was almost given away, along with the free theatre tickets. It was there I became addicted to London in general, and theatre in particular.

Cut back to the rear of the Rolls Royce where we were comfortably seated. I pleaded my ignorance to Brian and we had a whirlwind tour of the city, followed by coffee at NEMS, the record shop that Brian was running.

'Have you photographed the Beatles?' he asked. Again I was forced to reply in the negative.

'I was too tired.'

I'd had my chance in Birmingham the previous month, photographing an article on the young ladies of that town . . . a sort of 'Birds of Birmingham' photo-story. I'd run into a large screaming crowd of hysterical teenagers, waving banners and chanting, 'We want the Beatles, we want the Beatles . . .' The pavement was packed solid and they were held back only by a human chain of British bobbies. I had my cameras with me and took a few shots of the crowd. Suddenly a voice from a window above yelled out, 'Hey you!'

I looked up and saw a youngish man leaning out shouting at me. 'Do you want to photograph the Beatles?' It was then I realised I was in front of a broadcasting station. 'They're coming at five o'clock,' he yelled. 'Come back then. Tell the commissionaire I said it was OK. I'll meet you in the recording studio.'

He gave me his name and I pushed my way through the crowd to get to my next appointment. It turned out to be a very hectic session and it was only later in my hotel when I sat down with a pot of coffee to unwind, that I realised how absolutely whacked I was. I'd been working since the early hours of the previous morning and I really needed a rest. I couldn't jeopardise my obligations for what was really a self-indulgent exercise, no matter how tempting. Epstein listened to my explanations. 'As you didn't photograph the Beatles, you'd better photograph my new group when I visit London next month. I'll contact you.'

He spent the next few days taking me on a magical mystery tour of Liverpool. He was the perfect host. We visited the Cavern, the original home of the Beatles and of many other aspiring pop groups. Epstein was immediately recognised and mobbed by the crowd of very young fans who demanded his autograph. We literally had to fight our way out.

A visit to his parents' home proved just as arduous. On entering the house I was attacked by their miniature poodle, which fastened itself to my leg and immediately began to copulate furiously with it. I pretended to ignore it and with a fixed smile on my face acknowledged the introductions that were being conducted by Brian. With my other leg I tried to dislodge the black horror, but each time my free leg approached him, he would yap his head off and renew his activities with increased vigour. It was quite a feat trying to keep my balance while hacking away with my unviolated leg and at the same time shaking hands with Mrs Epstein, who looked down at the dog and said, with a beatific smile, 'Oh look, he's trying to tell you he likes you.'

Later we drove to a home, which to my surprise was very modest and sparsely furnished. I didn't enquire whether it was Brian's home or whether it belonged to the young man who was already ensconced on the settee. We'd hurried there to catch a TV program Brian wanted to watch and after introducing me to his companion, they both avidly discussed the program as it progressed, with me busy clicking away in the background.

The next day it was the docks and a ride up and down the Mersey on the ferry, then the slums and the controversial new cathedral. Last but not least was the film studio where they were shooting *Ferry Across the Mersey* with Gerry and the Pacemakers, another one of his groups.

All the while I was snapping away. We went on the set where he introduced me to all and sundry, including Cilla Black. 'Don't be bloody silly Brian, we know each other,' she said. A few months before, Cilla had come to my studio for a session and we'd got to know each other quickly because of mutual friends. One of these was an old school chum of hers who had become a sort of musical agent. He'd wanted to sign her up but Brian had got in first.

I arrived back in London with lots of pictures which the magazine wanted immediately. My own schedule was very tight and as it would save me a tedious stint in the dark-room, I agreed to let them have the negatives. I never got them back and forgot all about them until over a quarter of a century later when I needed a print for my exhibition at the National Portrait Gallery. Luckily I still had a few proof enlargements which I'd printed prior to their dispatch.

Brian phoned me on his next visit to London as promised and I did a session with him and the new group, outside the London Palladium, the Mecca of showbiz. The group did not make too much of an impact and certainly never made a successful pilgrimage to this shrine, and for all intents and purposes, died a death.

Brian, who did make an impression on this same scene, also died a death, but for different reasons.

beyond the fringe...

Satirical conundrum—

QUESTION:

When does four of a kind and a full house make a Royal flush?

ANSWER:

Any night at the Fortune Theatre when the Queen can get a seat.

It is well over a quarter of a century since *Beyond the Fringe* hit London. It was a blitzkrieg by a company of four, Peter Cook, Dudley Moore, Jonathon Miller and Alan Bennett. Devastation lay in the wake of their accurate bombardment of 'the Establishment'. To say 'Pooh' to enshrined heroes like Douglas Bader was obscene, and to depict him tottering on tin legs and mouthing prep school platitudes about bringing down enemy airmen during the Battle of Britain was sacrilege of the highest order. Like the original Blitz, *The Fringe* shattered the face of theatrical London forever.

Post-war, a new style of architecture had arisen from the ashes of London. Whether it was good or bad was debatable. It depended on the taste of the architects. Bugger the public!

Phoenix-like, *The Fringe* rose from the smouldering corpses of the sacred cows that had been accurately targeted and destroyed. A new breed of satirists took over and occupied the scene. Fledglings from this Mother-Phoenix, they filled the vacuum left by the firestorm that had consumed Victorian values. Like post-war architecture, a lot of traditions were ruthlessly and sometimes mindlessly eliminated. Whether this was desirable depended on the tastes of the satirists. Bugger the public!

I took the front-of-house photographs for *Beyond the Fringe* in 1961. Discussing the review with the producer, Willy Donaldson, I decided that to keep the irreverent tone of the show, I too would break with tradition. So I shot the entire front-of-house pictures in various unlikely locations—in and around Regent's Park, and then actually in the Zoo itself, Hampstead Heath and London telephone booths. In Brighton we used the bus depot, an itinerant harpist busking in the High Street, the beach, the promenade and the boys clambering in and out of dodgem cars. They squatted on the famous breakwater, seated themselves in striped deckchairs on the famous pier and balanced or hung from the black painted girders supporting it. The photos showed the cast in situations which had nothing whatsoever to do with the show.

It's easy to be clever after the event but the whole point of filming them in the street was that there was nothing to shoot on stage. It was all words and only twice were the lads in anything other than their normal clothes. Richard Lester had a similar problem with the Beatles. He had four chaps and what could they do? Sing. So what could he get them to do but . . . goon around? To goon around in a background is better than gooning around in four walls.

For the production itself the boys were dressed in dark grey slacks and matching long-sleeved sweaters. There were only the two costume changes. In the first, for a skit on television commercials, they were clad, head to toe, in yellow oilskins, sou'westers and gumboots. In the other, a Shakespearian sketch, they donned a variety of hats, helmets and crowns, and were issued with swords. All except Dudley Moore, who, being a musician, clutched a lute, a pig's bladder and wore a jester's cap. These props were very photogenic so I photographed the boys in them, hamming it up for publicity purposes. Subsequent photo-calls by other photographers tended to latch onto these same two situations. As the photos proved very popular and received extensive media exposure, I kept to my original front-of-house intentions. These images never graced the frames in front of the theatre.

I think the boys were aware of their power at the time. It was the first time that anybody had had the nerve to come out in public and demolish those sacred cows, our 'beloved institutions'. Pete and Dud came from a middling sort of background, but Jonathon Miller was a doctor from a wealthy Jewish family. They'd all met at Cambridge and had been part of *The Footlights Revue*. Alan Bennett came from a more working-class background and still had a bit of a North Country accent, but he exuded a gentility. He'd been to Oxford, where he later became a don.

There'd always been satire of sorts, but it was usually restricted to things like *Punch*, where it was a much more intellectual thing. With *The Fringe*, satire was being brought directly to the public and it penetrated quite different stratas; it even got onto television, with Pete and Dud still satirising 'the Establishment'. It spawned a new wave in satire with 'That Was The Week That Was', 'Sorry—I'll Say that Again', 'Monty Python's Flying Circus' and 'The Goodies'. The list goes on. The spores spread overseas, resulting in a rash of foreign imitators, following what seemed to be the new tradition, 'No Rules is Good Rules'. It reached a tremendous public and in the process became much broader, more anarchistic. *The Fringe* was more cerebral, but 'Python' went beyond that—blowing things up. *The Fringe* was much more subtle, but you get to the point where people get used to subtlety and then you've got to go beyond it.

the new 'Establishment'...

The stupendous success of *The Fringe* was closely followed by another. Peter Cook, with Nick Luard, created The Establishment, a satirical nightclub in the former premises of the Soho strip club, La Tropicana, right in the middle of theatreland. Peter asked me if I would like to move in. My existing space at Panaramic Studios was rather cramped, with no room to swing a one-tailed mouse in, let alone a cat-of-nine. 'Yes!' I cried, and literally did with joy, when I saw the space. It was fantastic. Four floors! The basement was to be Dudley's jazz cellar while the ground floor was to be the club proper, with its adjoining bar and stage. I had the first floor, a vast area which I divided into darkrooms and a large reception/office. There was plenty of studio space left, enough to do crowd scenes. I later took advantage of this situation when tackling some television and advertising assignments.

Sean Kenny, the architect and stage designer who had created the designs for *Beyond the Fringe* and *Oliver* had the second floor. The top floor was vacant, originally designated for storage, but not for long.

The membership of the club grew with unprecedented rapidity and was appreciated by all concerned. But space was now a problem. There was only one solution. Peter approached me and said in that funny Dud and Pete voice, 'If I offered you one million pounds, would you move to the top floor?'

I realised immediately that although the offer was not serious, the request was. Peter had resorted to his 'Wisty' voice to cover his embarrassment. I had only just settled in after the hectic building of darkrooms, office and reception, the rewiring and new plumbing and installation of telephones. I was physically and financially depleted. Nevertheless, I complied and moved my studio. It turned out for the better as now I wouldn't be getting so many inquisitive, unwanted callers, who had been following their noses and the shared staircase from the club up to my studio entrance. There was now the buffer of Sean's studio between me and the club, and by the time they had reached Sean's floor, the idea of coping with another two flights rapidly diminished their curiosity. The ground floor space had been adequate for the club's initial needs, but the membership explosion was totally unexpected and the subsequent solution advantageous to all. The club paid for the expenses of my move and everyone was happy.

It was one big happy family. Well, at least for a while. But like all families it grew and changed. And the changes were not always for the better.

standing room only...

When The Establishment first opened, it was such a success that people had to be turned away. The membership outstripped the facilities. People queued for hours to get in, and when they did, they had to queue again for drinks. The waiters were run off their feet. It was almost impossible to attend the performances in the minute theatre, where the seating consisted of wooden benches which people climbed on to get a better view, thus defeating the purpose of them being there at all. It was standing room only.

The already small auditorium was later converted into a theatre/dining room which left it without any standing room whatsoever. It was a task of devout dedication to attend a performance. Years later I reminisced with Barry Humphries who recalled with horror his encounter with that infinitesimal stage.

I saw nearly all the shows that played there. I didn't have to pay as I was part and parcel of the place. The revues were sensational as well as unconventional. Frankie Howerd was brought out of obscurity, dusted and pushed onto the miniscule boards to stutter his way to a new lease of life, a resurrection that would have made Lazarus envious.

Lenny Bruce's appearance shocked 'the establishment' at The Establishment. *The Fringe* had gone down quite well in America, but with nothing like the impact they'd had in England. In certain respects the humour did not translate. But Bruce's language, replete with four-letter words, was universal. Police in mufti, so it was said, attended the opening night's performance and rumours of them raiding the dressing-room, along with rumours of forbidden drugs, were rife.

Forbidden words and subjects were amalgamated into a nightly paean of liberated perceptions, with Bruce's performance the purgative to the inhibitions of the packed audience. I think the war had a lot to do with it. One had accepted an awful lot of stuff because one didn't want to be disloyal. One wanted to be patriotic. But by the 1960s one had got to the point of saying, 'Bugger it!'

Bruce's liberal use of the four-letter word, interspersed with observations about the derivations of 'sperm', 'faeces', 'vagina', 'penis' and 'masturbation', certainly unclogged the constipated minds of many of the so-called sophisticates.

Within the four walls of the club, these words made sense. Once outside, they were hurriedly fed into the maw of the media, which never considered masticating, let alone digesting the message behind the words. Instead they indignantly spewed them out, half-chewed, onto the front pages of the tabloids in banner headlines, with some of the letters asterisked to make them palatable to their regular readers, people who used these terms as a matter of course in their daily conversation. They were words which if eliminated from their vocabulary would have rendered them totally inarticulate.

John Bird, Eleanor Bron, Jeremy Geidt and John Fortune, the resident cast of The Establishment, were very articulate without resorting to anything more shocking than the occasional 'damn!' Very British, none of your Yankee overkill here. Nevertheless, both Lenny Bruce and 'the Stabbers' cast', as they were known, each in their own ways, successfully carried out their objectives.

Private Eye…

Willy Donaldson was a public school boy, like many of the others connected with the satire boom. He'd gone to Cambridge from Winchester and it was at university that he met Peter Cook and some of the people who worked for *Private Eye*. Peter was connected to *Private Eye* as well, so once I'd moved into The Establishment I got quite friendly with them. I started doing covers for the magazine and even did a book with Willy Rushton and Roy Hudd, *How to Play Football*, but it was a disaster commercially.

One day, a young man appeared in my studio. 'Peter Cook said that if I told you I was a friend of his, you'll take my photograph.' It was David Frost. This led to a meeting with Ned Sherrin, the producer of 'That Was The Week That Was', on which Frost was appearing. So I came to do all the stills for the program, and a book of the series, and was one of the first photographers to get screen credit. That in turn led me to work on 'Not So Much A Programme, More a Way of Life', and also, numerous publications for the BBC.

not 'in' with the 'in' crowd…

Peter Cook, much to the disappointment of many of the members, rarely made an appearance at The Establishment, but Dudley Moore was there nearly every night, playing jazz in the basement. More often than not the only way to hear Dud's trio was to stand outside in the street and listen to the music escaping through the window grills, where the windows had been left wide open to help ventilate the overcrowded, Calcutta-like hole. I used to go down after I'd finished working and do a bit of twisting. Almost my whole social life revolved around The Establishment, apart from some old friends from art school days.

The members, in more ways than one, stood for all the inconveniences because it was the 'in' place, the place to be seen. Everyone who was 'someone' went to The Establishment. You had to go at least once to say that you'd been.

That I happened to have my studio at a place where such a lot of people congregated, and that I happened to be a photographer meant that I became a part of it all. But I think I stood apart from the 'in' crowd. It's an awful thing which I've had all my life, of wanting to achieve something on my own merits, not because of who I know, and yet I have been a bit too lazy to really push myself to the limit. Things happened to me and though I felt I wasn't really responsible, it meant that I happened to be in the swim.

The 'in' places were mostly private parties, sometimes fashion shows, the ultimate being a party given by a fashion designer. Photographers were 'in' as well as certain types of theatre people and all the paraphernalia of the swinging sixties. But I was never really a part of that, even though I'd occasionally end up at the parties of people like Miranda, a doyenne of the swingers. It was not really my scene. I didn't drink, I didn't take drugs.

There were three or four well-known restaurants in the vicinity of The Establishment which were places to be seen in. Wheeler's, a seafood restaurant, The Trattoria Terrazza, which was full of actors and actresses, and Ronnie Scott's, the jazz club. The Escargot, a French restaurant right opposite The Establishment, was quite 'in' but the one I went to more was an 'Italian' restaurant next door, called Romano Santi. It was filled with actors and actresses of the humbler and 'resting' ranks because you could have a three-course meal there for five shillings, and this was at a time when a meal elsewhere might cost you between 25 and 30 shillings. In the evening it was more expensive. It was faded plush inside and the waiters served you in dinner jackets, a little the worse for wear. It had been a very good restaurant but had become down at heel and although it had an Italian name, I think it was run by Maltese.

Another great place further away from Soho was Schmidt's. There was a sort of delicatessen underneath and a restaurant on top. There, one was served by German waiters who must have escaped before the war because they were, by then, about 70 years old. Bertorelli's was another well-known place and Sheekie's was a fish place down the road. Then there were cafes for art students and music afficionados, where people like Tommy Steele performed 'The Two I's'.

There was a place called The Revolution which I occasionally visited. There they had rock bands, and light shows generated by a simple projector, projecting a mixture of oil and paint, spliced between glass slides. The heat made the mixture bubble and this created the psychedelic effects. One could judge how long a place had been in operation by the condition of the projector, which became encrusted with a hideous mess, while an ever-increasing stain spread across the floor in front.

In general though, I didn't go to pop concerts or listen to pop music. I found most of the lyrics banal and much preferred people like Frank Sinatra, Ella Fitzgerald and Count Basie. I was really much more interested in food and sometimes theatre.

Miranda's house...

Miranda was the closest I ever got to someone who was, in their own way, living out the myths of the sixties. She was the only friend I was aware of who was using heroin. One would find random people in her house in varying stages of intoxication, lying on a couch, tripping on LSD, smoking hash, and on one occasion, a blonde with her skirt up, pleading with her negro boyfriend to give her a 'hit'. I watched while she was being shot-up with heroin and all the while Miranda was looking at a proof sheet of photos, saying 'I'll have that one, and that one.'

I didn't relate to drugs. It was not that I was against them as such, but I had no interest in altered states. For me, that would not have been living a true moment.

sitting pretty... Christine Keeler...

My own driving force has always been more emotional than intellectual and so the sixties was also *my* period in that sex became the great leveller. People had always experimented but in the sixties it was done openly.

When Christine Keeler was paid some substantial amount of money to give her story to the newspapers, such things became common knowledge. She had been sleeping with John Profumo, the Minister for War in the Macmillan Government and Eugene Ivanov, a Russian diplomat, at the same time, and so what is now known as 'The Profumo Affair' broke. Profumo resigned his post and the Government was brought into chaos and disrepute, and another of 'our beloved institutions', this time a central one like the Government, turned to dust.

She was, I think, without political ideas or motivations, an innocent pawn with perhaps no greater wish than to have a good time. She was a girl who started out as a stripper and was suddenly being taken to all the best parties by her new posh friends. They were having their 'bit of rough' while she indulged in her Cinderella fantasy and became a victim of the situation, with everyone looking to make capital out of her.

Her Svengali was the society osteopath, Stephen Ward, who knew everyone, the toffs and the riffraff, and it was he, I believe, who was moving the chess pieces.

I only met Christine twice. Once when she was brought to my studio above The Establishment to be photographed for a film about her life, and then again, when she came the next day to look at the proofs.

The circumstances behind the publication of the photographs I took that day, arose from inside information and secret agreements involving people either in, or close to the Government, the Opposition, and of course entrepreneurs after a quick buck and journalists after a quick scoop. I was caught up in the sticky web when one of the photographs I had taken was 'borrowed' and sold without my permission to a Sunday tabloid.

When Christine Keeler was brought to my studio I was expecting a pretty hard bill of goods. The girl that faced me was anything but that. Here was a woman, slightly bewildered or perhaps intoxicated by all the publicity surrounding her recent exploits. I was going to use the expression, 'wide-eyed innocence' but I think 'wide-eyed naivety' might be nearer the truth. One felt that the whole matter had got out of hand.

Whether the rumours of espionage and blackmail that linked the players in this bedroom farce were valid, I am in no position to say. I do not wish to speculate and add to the fictions or factions of the Profumo Affair. My concern with the scandal was restricted to the use and misuse of the photographs I took of Christine Keeler, if not the main, then the most publicised protagonist in the pot-pourri of press, politics, prostitutes and police.

Someday I hope there will be a satisfactory explanation of the truths, half-truths and downright lies that have surrounded these photographs of Christine Keeler, and perhaps even those that have plagued Christine herself.

in a nutshell...

The following is a condensed version of a long and tedious saga which I will try my best to convey as briefly as possible.

Christine Keeler was brought to my studio by an associate, and the producers of a film company that he had got himself involved with. They wanted photographs of her to publicise a proposed film of the 'Affair'. Here was one of the principal pieces in a game of power and politics, who was also a pawn, but who had the capacity to threaten the Queen, the Bishops and the Knights *and* bring down the castles of the establishment.

Nude shots of Keeler were wanted to highlight the sexual implications for those captured in this web of intrigue. Keeler was reluctant to pose naked and after several innocuous cheesecake positions, the film company representatives insisted on her carrying out their contractual requirements. There was an impasse which I solved by clearing the studio of people, including my assistants. 'If it's required for you to pose naked,' I said to her, 'then we can do it, without showing what they want to see. Take off your clothes and sit back to front on that chair. Most of you will be hidden but you will have carried out their conditions.'

I turned my back while she stripped and straddled the chair. Then I shot off a role of film in a matter of minutes, asked her to get dressed and that was the end of the session. The next day she came to see the results and was pleased with the solution to her dilemma.

I did a series of enlargements for the film company to use as pre-production shots. My associate, whom I will call 'Mick', said, 'You can use the pictures as we need publicity for the film.'

One of the shots was lying on my desk when a young man, who introduced himself as a friend of my partner, walked into the studio some time later. He said he'd been told of the photographs I'd taken of Keeler. At this time, interest in the scandal was reaching epic proportions, and anything connected with it was 'hot' property.

I showed him the photograph and he raved about it, asking if he could take it to show a friend and promising to return with it immediately. He didn't. What he did, in fact, was to sell it to the *Sunday Mirror*.

I was flabbergasted when he told me and immediately phoned the newspaper to tell them that they could not publish the picture. It was too late, I was told, the photo had already gone to press.

On publication I was threatened with legal action by the film company for selling the picture without their permission. The explanation I gave did not exonerate me. They said I was responsible for the photographs.

I contacted 'BeeJay', the young man who had sold the photo without my permission. 'Don't worry,' he said. 'It'll be OK.'

The following day I received a phone call, telling me to go to the offices of David Jacobs, QC. He was later to represent the Beatles. On meeting Jacobs, I told him my side of the story, including 'Mick's' permission to use the shots. 'Ring Mick now and ask him to put it in writing,' Jacobs said. I did so while Jacobs listened with a single headphone attachment held to his ear. 'Remember when I took the pictures,' I said, 'you told me I could make use of them?'

'Yes,' he answered.

'Could you put it in writing for me please?' There was a pause. 'I'll get back to you,' he said and hung up.

As I replaced the receiver a man walked into Jacobs' office, nodding his head. Jacobs beamed. 'Make an appointment with the film company and Mick,' he told me. 'My clerk was listening on the other extension and heard the whole conversation.'

A meeting was arranged and Jacobs informed me that he would sit in the car and not make an appearance until all were present. Everyone was there, excepting Mick. I told them that the meeting could not take place until Mick arrived. After numerous phone calls he was tracked down and joined us. I went down to the car and returned with Jacobs.

As we walked in there was an agitated stir among those present. 'You bastard!' one of them hissed at me. 'How did you get him?' It wasn't until then that I realised how important Jacobs was. I had told him that I did not have the means to make use of his services but he had told me not to worry. Evidently 'BeeJay' had some arrangement with him.

Sitting down, Jacobs called out Mick's name, with a quizzical glance around the room. When Mick identified himself Jacobs spoke again. 'Sir, did you, or did you not give Mr Morley permission to make use of the pictures as he deemed fit? Yes or No?' Without hesitation to allow any time for Mick to reply, Jacobs continued. 'Before you answer, I must tell you that I have categorical proof that you did.'

There was a stunned silence and Mick hesitantly muttered. 'Well . . . I . . .' and stopped.

'Gentlemen,' said Jacobs, looking around him as he rose to his feet, 'I think that answers my question.'

He turned and left the room without a further word. The silence was broken by one of the others. 'Mick! You lied to us!'

Although the film was subsequently abandoned, the pictures were in great demand and I decided that they should be syndicated through a picture agency, known to me through Shura. The arrangement was that the proceeds should be split equally, three ways. One third to Christine, one third to the film company and one third to me. 'BeeJay' took 50 per cent of my share as his 'cut'. I cared less about the money than I did about the resolution of the legal entanglement.

Some months later, certain developments caused me to sever any business ties with 'BeeJay' and I told the picture agency that I wanted my negatives of Keeler back and did not want them used any more. They were reluctantly returned. By this time the whole Keeler episode was over and done with and lay dormant until I left the UK in 1971, to live in Australia.

Then, in the late 1970s, the Keeler images started popping up once more. The scandal was for some reason once more newsworthy and like a hidden chancre, it started to erupt again.

I wrote to the owner of the picture agency, demanding the reason for the use of the picture which I had asked to be withdrawn. I received no reply.

Soon the pictures were surfacing elsewhere, even on the cover of a French magazine, which I happened to see while on an assignment in Paris. The agency had not contacted me or sent any royalties. I wrote once more and again the answer was the same, no reply.

On my next assignment to the UK I made my way to the agency and confronted the owner, telling him that it was not the money so much as the way my requests had been disregarded that displeased me. He told me it was impossible to retrieve all the pictures that had been syndicated and in any case, he now had full rights to them, which 'BeeJay' had given him in return for a lump sum.

The other loser in this sad saga was Christine herself, who had not received any of the money due to her. I had heard that she was in financial straits and now suggested that she be paid any monies owing her to date. This also fell on deaf ears.

I was livid, telling him he knew 'BeeJay' had no rights to them. I held the negatives and I had not been informed of the transaction. I wanted a confrontation with the three of us and then he dropped another bombshell. 'BeeJay' was dead. '*Well*,' I thought, '*let sleeping dogs lie, or in this case, lying dogs sleep*.'

All was quiet for some time until the late 1980s when a new version of the formerly vetoed film was produced. Once more my picture of Christine exploded onto the screen, this time accompanied by a version of the pose, modelled by the actress who was playing Keeler in the film.

The one saving grace of this unsavoury sequence of events in my career was when once again coincidence took control. The National Portrait Gallery in London had two years previously decided to give me a retrospective, one-man show, scheduled for 1989.

It opened at the height of public interest in the recycled Keeler affair, with the much publicised film and the globe-trotting television appearances of the born-again celebrity. No doubt a large part of the massive attendance at the exhibition was generated by the current hype surrounding anything to do with the 'Affair'. And there was the image again, this time used on the posters to advertise the exhibition.

If fame and fortune are the prerequisites of a successful endeavour, then the Keeler photograph, on the scales of success, may have weighed a little light on the fortune side, but quite generously loaded on the fame pan.

The final irony lies in the fact that the film company never honoured my bill for the sitting they had commissioned.

icons...

I don't want to take total credit for this image of Christine Keeler. It has become a kind of icon, a legend that feeds on itself.

So many of the people we think about, whether they are writers, or artists, or politicians, or so-called ordinary people, we think about in terms of images, of what they look like. When one thinks of Oscar Wilde or Noel Coward, one thinks of an image of those men rather than of an impression derived from the lines they have written.

People like Christine Keeler or Marilyn Monroe, whose images are splashed all over the place, become part of the public memory, part of the public mind, and the public worships them as a believer might worship the icons in a Greek Orthodox church.

Keeler and Monroe represent the dreams of so many women and the desires of so many men. Once a person is recognised, identifiable, the legend builds up and detaches itself from the individual.

With Christine Keeler much was made of the fact that so many men had access to her, government ministers, diplomats, society gentlemen, perhaps even royalty itself. And in my photograph she was there, but she was hidden. There was this little covering that made her perhaps more desirable. If you whipped it away you would see what the high and mighty had seen, and you'd participate in their fantasy.

But this is hindsight. I used the chair for reasons I have explained elsewhere. I didn't create what that picture came to represent. It was a record and it achieved its prominence for extraneous reasons, not because of me.

when Caine was able... Michael Caine...

The settling in period was over. We had moved to The Establishment and all was ready to go, except we had not, as yet replaced our Miss Hounslow.

One day, a young actress was sitting in my office when I rang the employment agency for a secretary. She made frantic hand signals for me to terminate the call. 'You want a secretary?' she said when I hung up the phone. '... got the perfect one for you, she's looking for a job at this moment and she's very good.' That's how I met Michael Caine.

The new secretary was a girl called Penny, one of a trio of inseparables—Penny, Gay and Anneke—the *enfants*, not too *terribles*, of showbiz. They were permanent fixtures at The Establishment and could be seen every night in the basement, listening to Dudley Moore. During the day they wandered around the club, mixing with the actors and actresses who were between rehearsals or auditions, having a quiet drink at the bar.

I had my fair share of people traipsing up from the club to have coffee in my studio, whether I was there or not. It became a sort of unofficial meeting place, which was starting to get out of hand and out of coffee. Fortunately this stopped when I moved my studio to the top floor to allow for the club's expansion.

I was in the studio one morning when a tall, lean lad, dressed in blue jeans, put his head around the door. 'Is Penny here?' he said.

'In the office,' I gestured, 'go on in.'

I carried on marking some contacts for blowing-up, when in a few minutes came the inevitable question. 'Want some coffee?' yelled Penny.

'OK,' I replied, and ambled into the office where three mugs now stood steaming on the desk.

I noticed the young man's eyes as he leant over to pick up his mug. The eyelashes were quite blond and gave the slightest impression of an albino. He had fair hair and fair skin but was far from colourless. There was something of a chameleon about him, a personality of contradictions. He exuded an easy-going attitude but one was aware that there was more to him than surface charm, perhaps the slightest hint of confrontation—a sense of 'Don't take too many liberties mate!' All the indications of an interesting actor.

Penny introduced him as a very good friend and a very good actor . . . Mike . . . Michael Caine. He had a very pronounced East End accent with an irrepressible core of wit that kept breaking through his spiel. Unbeknown to us all, he was on the brink of becoming a superstar.

I cannot vouch for the truth of the following story, as it is something I never broached with him. It was told to me by one of his close cronies who was in the same film, the film that was about to launch him.

There was a bunch of young, talented hopefuls who were doing bits and pieces, hoping for a break and Mike was one of these. Casting was in progress for a film called *Zulu* and there was a part for which every Cockney lad in the business would give his eyeteeth. Mike went for it but was told by Stanley Baker, who was involved with the production, as well as starring in the film, that it had already been cast. Jimmy Booth had got it.

Disappointed, Mike asked if there wasn't a part available that he could do. No, he was told, the only part left was that of a young, upper-crust English officer. They had wanted James Fox, but he was unavailable. Now they were looking for an alternative.

'How about me?' suggested Mike. Baker wasn't impressed and scoffed at the idea, but Mike insisted that he could do it and pleaded for a chance to prove it. Baker gave him that chance and the rest is history.

I met up with Mike again when I photographed James Saunders's play, *Next Time I'll Sing to You*. Mike had very good notices but had to be replaced when he took his first starring role in *The Ipcress File*.

Once again he came before my lens as Sean Kenny was given the job of designing the production and asked me to take some portraits of Mike for that purpose.

For Michael Caine, lift-off had been achieved and he was rocketing up to join the English constellation of stars that included Sean Connery, Albert Finney and Peter O'Toole. That first cup of coffee my secretary gave him stood me in good stead.

As his star grew brighter, more and more photographs of him were needed. He was hailed as the new sex symbol, the epitome of Len Deighton's Harry Palmer, gazing through heavy, horn-rimmed spectacles. He inverted the Dorothy Parker couplet to a feminist maxim... 'girls always make passes at boys who wear glasses'.

Now that he was a sought-after commodity, it was hard to arrange sessions. I had already photographed him for several magazines I worked for, and felt guilty about taking advantage of his good nature. But once more I was asked by yet another magazine to get a photograph of him. I phoned him, apologising for having to ask him yet again, and hoping he didn't mind.

'Lewis,' he replied, in his down-to-earth way, 'the day you stop asking, that's the day I'll mind.'

changing voices...

The sixties witnessed this breaking down of class. Many of the new fashion photographers were working-class boys, who previously might only have been allowed to do newspaper work. And who had written plays previously? Well-educated, ex-university types, now supplemented or supplanted by the angry young men, many of whom were working-class, writing plays for working-class actors. This created the curious phenomenon of good actors, ex-public school types, putting on Cockney accents to take the part of a Cockney, and people like Michael Caine taking the part of upper-crust officers and so forth. The boundaries were becoming blurry.

a sporting chance... Lindsay Anderson...

It is to Shura that I owe my first taste of theatre photography. Shura knew everyone and everyone knew Shura. He was a fast-talking extrovert, a charming, though exasperating opportunist, constantly hatching impossible schemes that I was inadvertently a party to. Not having the moral courage or the physical stamina to combat his persuasive cajoling, I agreed, on this occasion, to photograph a Royal Court poetry reading, in spite of the fact that this assignment would probably be no more successful than many of Shura's other ventures.

Those taking part included Christopher Logue, reading his own poetry, ably assisted by an actor whose more than average size proboscis protuded from beneath a stygian thatch of curly hair and above a mouth from which issued a loud, Irish tirade. He reminded me of an attenuated version of Brendan Behan. His name was Peter O'Toole.

During that performance at the Court, I am sure he was unaware of the phenomenal international status that lay a few short years ahead, when he exploded on the screen, complete with bleached hair and a shortened nose, as Lawrence of Arabia.

Lindsay Anderson was the director of that Sunday night poetry reading and when Shura's article with my accompanying photographs failed to find a publisher, Shura decided to show the photographs to his old friend.

Lindsay asked to meet me, declaring himself impressed with the photographs and inviting me to attend a rehearsal he was conducting, and to bring my camera.

I turned up at the Royal Court as arranged and found myself on stage with Lindsay, surrounded by the cast, which included

Frank Finlay and Ian Bannen. Lindsay said I could shoot wherever and whatever I liked, as long as I didn't get in the way and hold up the action.

This was my first taste of stage photography and I am forever indebted to Lindsay for his sensitivity in allowing me full rein. I don't know how I achieved my debut without upsetting all concerned, because looking at the results it is obvious I was very close in to the action, and in some shots, actually between the actors.

Bereft of experience and not really knowing how to tackle the problem I resorted to an instinctive solution, simply moving about at will, with no sense of formal posing. It developed into a working method for my front-of-house theatre photographs, later for television commercials, and with modifications, the style which I applied to most of my work where people are concerned.

I became one of the luckier photographers, with my own photo-calls, where the actors were going through their paces specifically for me. I attended rehearsals in advance, noting down the most photogenic scenes to be used in the front-of-house publicity. The actors worked naturally as I shot, avoiding the stiff posed pictures so often associated with the theatre.

Angus McBean's style of photography, beautifully posed and lit, was not for me. I was much more in line with what Tony Armstrong Jones was doing, where there was a rawness of presentation, using only available light. The result was technically grainy but for myself, and Armstrong Jones and a few others working in the genre, it seemed to suit the type of plays that were coming to the fore. They were angry plays in one way or another, all to do with the current social scene and people being buggered around. Using this more immediate technique, it didn't matter if the actor's face was half-obscured by the low lighting. Rather it added to the drama and seemed to reflect the very unvarnished view of human nature that was being presented in the play itself. No light domestic comedies where the girl had to look pretty and one had to start lighting up. It was as if the veneer on English society, firmly in place since it had been attached during the Victorian period, was starting to rub off. Theatre was a major part of that unstitching process. I succeeded, in a sense, because I wasn't in control of my medium. I had never trained as a photographer. I did not know my camera back to front, and I had to improvise.

In between taking pictures during that first rehearsal I had the opportunity to watch the way a play is structured. I saw 'notes' being given and discussions on the way a line should be delivered with the emphasis on certain words and the body language that complemented them. I watched Lindsay spend fifteen minutes convincing Alan Dobie that his way of approaching the line was the correct one, not Dobie's.

What my mind soaked up that afternoon was a distillation of theatre lore from a group of very dedicated and talented people and I learnt in those few hours more about the workings of the theatre than many would in months of treading the boards.

Lindsay was pleased with the pictures I had taken. The front-of-house photographs for this production had already been commissioned but he used one of the rehearsal shots for the programme and told me I would photograph the next play he directed. A promise he kept.

Billy Liar...

One afternoon not too long after, as I was walking up Regent Street I noticed a character leaning nonchalantly against the lamp standard, on the kerb near Austin Reed's. His hands were thrust deep into his jacket pockets and he was in earnest conversation with another, similarly clad person. Their peaked caps were pulled down over their eyes and I swerved to avoid passing too close as they looked like trouble. Before I had the chance to take another crab-like step, a hand shot out from the shorter of the duo and he pulled me towards him. I thought I was in for a fight and felt my legs buckling under me, but he lifted his head to meet my eyes and I was looking into the amused face of Lindsay Anderson.

'Hello Lewis,' he said, slapping me on the shoulder. 'I'm doing a new play and you're going to do the photographs!'

He hesitated for a moment. 'And *he*'s going to be in it,' he added, gesturing his thumb at the other man, who now held out his hand. 'Lewis Morley, Albert Finney,' said Lindsay, by way of introduction. I took the proffered hand as Lindsay continued. 'It's to be called *Billy Liar*.'

Billy Liar was the testing ground. It was my first attempt at front-of-house photography and it was my good luck that both the play and the photographs were a success. I had been thrown into the deep end without a life jacket in the grown-ups' pool of a major West End production. It was sink or swim and if I sank, it would be without a trace. The Royal Court where I had managed to keep my nose above water by dog-paddling, had given me some confidence and I struck out blindly for the side... any side. That I managed to pull myself out with creditable results meant I had joined the rat-race of theatrical photography where there are more eager hopefuls than there are rejected scripts.

I must admit I was more than a little nervous on this first engagement. I had attended some rehearsals and was now on familiar terms with the cast, which was halfway towards a successful session, but my way of working was a little disconcerting to some of the more established actors. I told them the scene I wanted to shoot and the point I wished to capture, asking the actors taking part to run through it and to ignore me. This went quite well until the crucial moment arrived when I tried to catch the action of Mona Washbourne, unselfconsciously pouring tea into a cup. Just as I was about to press the release on my camera, Mona, who was playing Albert Finney's mother, froze into position, holding the teapot as rigidly as her attitude.

'No Mona,' I admonished gently. 'Forget about me. Pour the tea into the cup, carry on talking to the others and forget about the camera.'

'But Angus always tells us to "hold it",' she replied.

'I'm not Angus,' I reminded her quietly and soon she was reacting in the way I wanted, as were the rest of the cast.

During its record run I shot *Billy Liar* at least eight times. The long run meant new photographs brought on by cast changes, as new members replaced the originals for one reason or another. Among these were Tom Courtney, who replaced Albert as Billy. Sometimes the reshuffling of the original cast necessitated another photo-call as people like Trevor Bannister, who played Billy's friend, replaced Tom Courtney in the title role.

I breathed a sigh of relief when I photographed the production for the last time for a provincial tour, its cast completely different from the opening night. This one play, photographed and rephotographed in the formative period of my theatrical photography, stood me in good stead for all the productions that followed, allowing me to swim confidently in the deep end.

I continued to photograph others of Lindsay's plays, including his National Theatre production of *Andorra* with Tom Courtney. Oscar Lewenstein, the producer of *Billy Liar* was impressed enough to commission me for his next production and to write me a letter of congratulation on the work I turned out for him. He gave me the bulk of his productions to photograph in the years that followed. Other managements used me and I enjoyed a blissful union with the theatre, photographing over 100 West End productions before I left for Australia in 1971.

I will forever be indebted to Lindsay for recognising my potential in the first few feeble efforts that were shown to him, and to Shura for all the wild-goose chases he led me into.

One of the photographs taken of Albert Finney for press publicity was Billy writing his name in chalk on the red brick wall facing the theatre. Twenty or more years later when Lindsay visited me in Australia, he astounded me with the news that the name was still there on the wall. On my next assignment in the UK I made a point of seeing it for myself. There it was, still writ bold, defying time and the elements. In the ensuing years I made the pilgrimage to the spot every time I visited London, each visit resulting in a fainter image than before.

On my last visit in 1989 I saw only the evidence of a few scraps of greyish, illegible chalk, clinging half-heartedly to the grimy, now almost blackened bricks. On my next visit I am certain that all vestiges of Billy's exuberant message will have disappeared, and with the changing face of London, maybe even the wall it was written on.

Tom Courtney...

Tom took over as Billy Liar from Albert Finney during the play's run at the Cambridge Theatre. Later, he appeared in the film version. I always found him retiring, quite shy and perhaps a little screwed-up. He didn't exude the confidence he must have had to be able to cope with the various roles that [illegible] successfully tackled.

I recall that I was rather puzzled by his naivety one night when he and John Thaw (later of 'The Sweeney' fame) were discussing a photograph I had on the wall of my studio.

John had dropped in to say hello and to see the results of his portrait session, but his attention was caught by a large print of a nude torso. It was so heavily textured by an induced grain that it had become almost abstract, very sixties.

'Must get Tom to see what he thinks,' he said, and rushed off downstairs to find him. He returned presently, dragging Tom behind him. John pointed in the direction of the photograph. 'Wotcha think of it?'

Tom stood for several seconds, staring at the print without making any comment. 'You know what it is, don't you?' questioned John, in exasperation.

Without taking his eyes off the image, Tom replied in a broad Midlands accent, 'Aye, it's a picture of a naked lady.'

'Strewth!' exploded John and pushed Tom out of the studio.

I had occasion to photograph Tom several times after that, among them, for Lindsay Anderson's production of *Andorra* at the National Theatre. There was also a special portrait for his interpretation of Hamlet, directed by Caspar Wreder, and a rather enjoyable romp through the back lanes of Soho for some other shots.

Years later, during one of my visits to the UK I went to see *The Dresser* with Tom in the name part and went backstage to say hello.

'Where have you been all these years?' he asked.

'In Australia,' I replied.

'Yes, I thought you had an Australian accent,' he said.

I was dumbfounded. Had I acquired an Australian accent? Nobody else had suggested as such or had Tom perceived a change in me that was unrecognised by others, even my family and close friends? Or was it once again that naivety taking over, as in the case of 'The Naked Lady'?

theatrical alchemy...

I was involved enough in the plays I photographed to read the text and go to rehearsals, sometimes two or three, to make up my mind what I wanted to shoot. To leave it to the run-through would be too close to the opening.

Something I noticed time and time again was that the intimacy and enthusiasm of the group of actors and others involved in the production of the play actually changed one's perception of the quality of the material. Sometimes one would read the text and think, *This is a bloody awful play!* Then one attended two or more rehearsals and there was this feeling of togetherness, enthusiasm, like a little family and one would think, *It's not bad. Everybody's enthusiastic about it.*

Then one would go to the first night, where all scales would fall from the eyes and leave one thinking, *Shit! It really is bad after all.*

a Speight worse than death...

When thinking of playwrights with musical aspirations, Woody Allen and his clarinet spring to mind, but very few people would associate Johnny Speight with the drums, as I do.

Speight is more readily associated with his creation of the loud, garrulous character, Alf Garnet, than with the hesitant flurries of uncoordinated breaks that assailed my ears during a special photographic session with him. He was more dexterous with his East End dialogue than he was with his drumsticks.

In 'Till Death Us Do Part' with Warren Mitchell and Dandy Nichols, the protagonists juggled with the words Speight tossed them, weaving them into a brilliant tapestry of dialogue. From Mitchell, hilarious, over-the-top bigotry and from Nichols, the subdued tones of a delicious, deflating put-down, letting the whole diatribe wash over her without apparent concern. It was a beautiful, underplayed performance.

Speight's agent wanted me to photograph him playing the drums for an article promoting a play which was just about to be unleashed on the West End. I had also been commissioned to photograph the front-of-house pictures.

The play received a very cool reception from both critics and public alike and Speight's reaction to the reception was rather like his drumming—sad.

I remember sitting in the back row of the stalls on the first night, aware of a heavy breathing presence behind me. Leaning on his elbows on top of the wooden curtain partition that ran along the last row of the seating, was Speight.

'Hello Lewis,' he whispered. I turned around and looked up at a face dimly lit by the glow of the exit lights above the double-swing doors, immediately behind us. 'I can't stand it!' he added. 'I'm going for a drink.'

He disappeared before I even had time to answer and I did not see him for the rest of the evening.

I found the play uneven but interesting in its subject matter and structure. It was pre-Orton but had a similar quirkiness which left you with the same sense of unease that Orton did. I have not been aware of a revival of *The Knacker's Yard* and I think the only satisfaction he got out of the debut, besides the thrill of seeing his play produced in a West End theatre, were the photographs from the front-of-house display. He was, to my satisfaction, very pleased with them and ordered an extra set for himself.

A few years later I happened to be staying in the same hotel as Speight. He was sitting at the bar, engrossed in his thoughts and the contents of the tumbler in front of him. It seemed he had entered a period that a lot of people connected with showbiz go through, an occupational hazard for many members of the profession. It is an ordeal to be faced alone, publicly or with a group, anonymously. Some were consumed, some were saved, some phoenix-like, were born again, only to be confronted with the same problem later. Rebirth, in these situations can become a habit, like the one they are trying to kick.

A very few seem to have discovered the secret of the fire walkers and emerge, unsinged. Speight was apparently one of those, for years later he was still turning out situation-comedies that not only hurt our sides with laughing but also our conscience, with the recognition of those qualities that Speight had seen in all of us.

overheard in the tobacconist's…

I used to pay three or four visits a day to the tobacconist next door to my studio, getting through, without too much help from my friends, three to four packs of cigarettes a day. By buying one pack at a time I felt that I was cutting down. Buying three packs in one fell swoop would be a sign of weakness, a foregone conclusion, an admission of defeat.

On one of these regular excursions I waited behind a couple of young waiters, one of whom worked in The Establishment, unavoidably eavesdropping on their conversation.

'They say his mate bashed his head in with a hammer, and the only way they could identify him was by the tattoo of a bird on his belly.'

'Didn't think he liked birds?'

'No, you prick . . . was one of them with wings.'

'You mean an angel?'

'Naw . . . a bloody swallow . . . you know what I mean.'

'Yeah! What's that they say? One swallow don't make a summer.'

'You can say that again.'

'Bet he had more than one swallow. Know what I mean?'

'Come off it! Show a bit of respect!'

They made their purchases and shuffled out. I think in a funny sort of way they had shown their respect, by knowing about him. Joe would probably have liked that. I returned to my studio, smoked a few cigarettes and wrote a poem about him. Joe Orton would have hated that.

portrait of the artist as a young man . . .

He was sprawled out on the front seat of the stalls, an odalisque, more mannered than a Matisse. His playing was just a little too method, a little too relaxed, hinting at a tension not quite overcome. His arms, which rested on the backs of the red velveteen seats, were encased in black leather, studded with chromium-plated, round-headed rivets, like those on an overstuffed Victorian settee. A matching black leather cap rounded off the outfit.

Who was this sheep in wolf's clothing? I mused. The aggressive attire seemed out of place. Here was a very young head on very young, one could almost say, delicate, shoulders.

His head was tilted back to take in the surroundings from the low vantage point he had assumed. He regarded me with

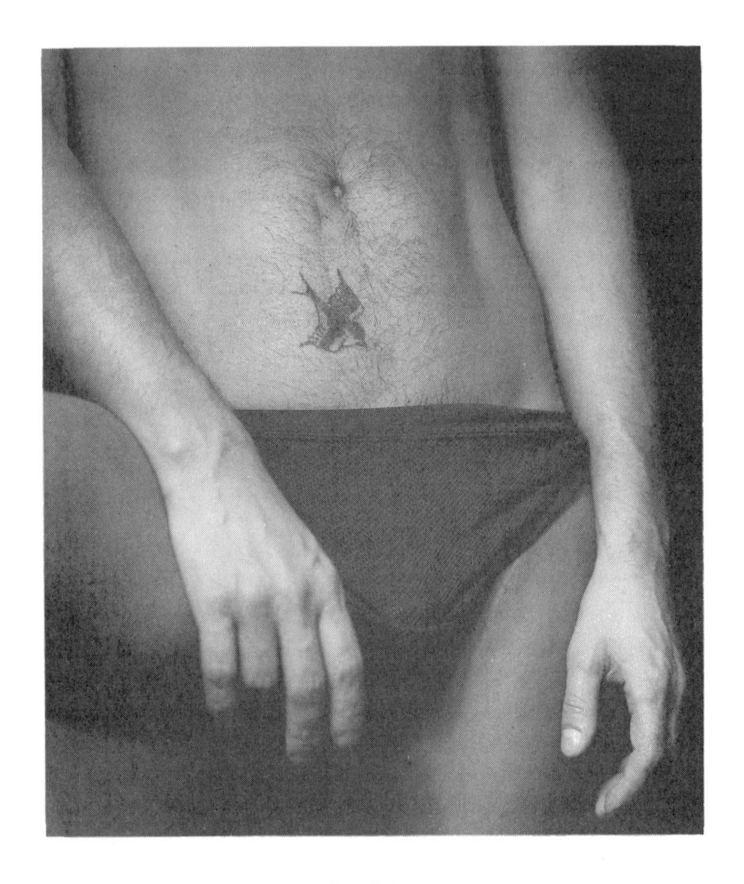

Joe Orton

a challenging stare from beneath the peak of the leather cap that sat forward on his brow, covering his forehead. The eyes were dark and shiny, beady . . . like an inquisitive fieldmouse. Still reclining, he held out his hand as we were introduced by Peter Wood, who was to direct the play Orton had written.

After a couple of muttered acknowledgments, he resumed his original position and I continued my discussion with the director concerning the front-of-house and publicity photographs for this, the first production of *Loot*.

If the names of the cast who were appearing in the production had been invented by Orton, I wouldn't have been surprised, excepting that they were established actors. Ian McShane, Geraldine McEwen, Duncan McCrae, John Batty and finally, the most bizarre member of the cast with the most ordinary name, Kenneth Williams. I was surprised the production hadn't been dubbed *McLoot*!

In later years, after the death of Orton, Kenneth Williams directed a more successful production of *Loot*, but this first production, like one of the characters in the play, died a death and was shuffled around, willy-nilly, for quite a while.

I had also photographed the first production of *Entertaining Mr Sloane*, at the Arts Theatre the previous year, without having met the author. Its favourable reception by both critic and public had ensured its transfer to a larger West End theatre, followed by a long run.

Prior to its proposed transfer and opening in the United States, I was asked to take some special publicity photographs of Joe. They were to be body-building type shots, as he wanted it to be known that he was the fittest, best built playwright in the western hemisphere. In the interrum I had met Orton at the *Loot* photo call.

I expected him to arrive with the usual body-building gear that one sees stretched over the highly oiled and over-developed muscles in the body-building magazines. The spangled jockstrap, the tiger-striped, hip-hugging, vee-cut costume. At least a pair of trendy, tight-fitting swimming trunks. When I was finally confronted by a slim youth, wearing a pair of ever-so-slightly stained Aertex underpants, I was ever-so-slightly shocked.

These days, when it is the norm to deliberately dress to shock, one isn't. Petticoats and bras worn as outer garments pass unnoticed. Underpants worn in the park raise not a furore or a giggle or even an eyebrow. But in the permissive sixties, which were still pretty stitched-up in more ways than one, to be photographed in underpants, other than for advertising, was tantamount to pornography. Like a Victorian pornographic photograph, where the male was often stark naked, except for a pair of socks, it provoked an unintentional air of hilarity.

I had misgivings about Joe's attire. I felt that the underpants would somehow make a joke of his intentions, but he appeared to be perfectly relaxed and completely at ease, exuding the confidence that what he had chosen for the session was absolutely right. I said nothing, feeling that any disapproval from me would be to no avail. It might unsettle and perhaps even hurt him. He did have a streak of vulnerability, I felt, very close to the surface.

It would have been easier to photograph him in the nude and pose him 'artistically' . . . meaning, hiding his cock. But as these photos were for promotional purposes in the United States, a fully naked figure posed the problem of censorship. Naked 'birds' showing their 'boobs' were OK, but naked guys showing their bums were definitely out. So, I did the best I could under the existing conditions.

It was our first meeting all over again. Joe wanted to be masculine and tough, fleshing out his biceps by pressing them against a closed fist. Lamb posing as ram. No way could he be compared to a marble Hercules, or a tanned Charles Atlas. He was more like the chap who had sand kicked in his face, or, to be fair, the comparison that sprang to mind was that of a Greek bronze of a youth, removing a thorn from his foot.

The session went without a hitch. In between cups of coffee and cigarettes he asked me about the paintings and sculpture hanging around the studio. I told him they were mine and that as I was more successful as a photographer than an artist, I only dabbled in my spare time. It was now a form of relaxation which helped me to wind down from the business of running a studio.

When Joe came to look at the contacts, he brought with him a large, framed collage, asking my opinion of it and whether I would like it. At our last meeting, he'd spoken about his brush with the law and the imprisonment resulting from his escapades with library books, where innocuous covers had been rendered scurrilous by some judiciously placed collaging. I didn't know whether to assume he'd done this larger collage or not. Not wanting to offend, I declined the offer in my gentlest manner, influenced no doubt by an aversion to the maltreatment of books which had arisen from my years in the prison camp.

He said nothing, neither justifying nor defending it. The only reaction was a slight droop of the shoulders. I felt that he wanted approval or at least some constructive criticism and not the lack of a response that I had given. He was pleased with the photos but nothing more was said about the collage and after a final cup of coffee he tucked the picture under his arm and left.

That was the last time I saw Joe although he did drop me a line ordering more prints and adding, 'America hated *Sloane*. We ran thirteen perfs. Ugh rotten Yanks! yours Joe. P.S. I'll pay for them naturally.'

When I read his diary and saw the film, *Prick Up Your Ears*, I was stunned as well as a little saddened, as my only recollections of him were of a gently spoken youth who housed a hidden sensitivity and vulnerability under the veneer of his brittle, devil-may-care attitude. But that may have been his strength, making use of his facility with words and his acute observations, changing rapidly as the situation demanded—the easy chameleon.

These many years later, knowing what I do now, I can only surmise that the collage was probably done by Kenneth Halliwell, Joe's lover, and that Joe was trying, in some way, to help him.

the young p.r.o. and the old pro... Margaret Leighton...

'Please may I come along?' Genista had just started working for Michael Codron as an assistant p.r.o. or public relations officer. Among other duties, her job was to send out press releases and photographs to publicise the plays Codron produced.

She had come to my studio to ask me if she could accompany me on a photo-call to take the front-of-house pictures for a new play. It was *The Girlfriend*, with Margaret Leighton in the lead.

If the whole world was a stage as Will Shakespeare would have it, then this little drama would be enacted, scripted with unrehearsed lines provided by circumstance and culminating in a really devastating curtain line, worthy of an Osborne or an Orton. It was the classic mould of a play within a play, with two leading ladies, one strutting the boards and the other providing the feed-lines off-stage.

I had already chosen the situations I intended to photograph from the rehearsals I had watched. The actors had been made aware of them and knew roughly the sequences to follow. In the case of photo-calls, these were more often dictated by costume changes than chronological order. Plays that had only one set of costumes were much easier to wrap up.

As usual, I arrived at the theatre twenty minutes to a half-hour before the arranged time when the cast, director and myself would gather to sort out the scenes and specify the actors to be used. This spare time was used to prepare the leads for my lighting, load my cameras and attend to all the small, time-consuming necessities. As I was doing this, Genista called out to me from the stool she was sitting on, off-stage in the wings.

'Lewis, how are you going to photograph Margaret Leighton?'

'What do you mean luv?' I replied.

'I mean how are you going to photograph her to make her look young? . . . I need pictures to publicise the show and it's going to be hard unless they are . . . well, you know what!'

'Don't worry,' I assured her. 'They'll be fine.'

'But she's so wrinkled,' persisted Genista.

'Look, she has a fabulous face and her cheekbones are marvellous. She's quite beautiful and very photogenic.'

'I hope you're right, this is my first job and . . .'

'Genista,' I pleaded. 'Don't worry! Wait until you see the photos, then you can make up your mind.'

I carried on while she sat, looking glum, not totally convinced by my assurances. Within the next few minutes, the range of expressions that she was to convey, acting out her reactions, were unfortunately not due to her acting ability.

'Hello Lewis, knew you were here,' quipped John Standing, one of the actors, as he strode onto the stage.

'How?' I queried.

'The mikes are on,' he smirked, turning slightly in the direction of Genista.

Looking over I saw the poor girl, fingers stuffed into her open mouth, a horrified expression on her face as the significance of those words sunk in.

On the skirting of the stage, a microphone is installed and connected to the dressing-rooms and other strategic points, so when a performance is in progress, the mike is left on, allowing the actors not actually on stage to be aware of their cues. Obviously someone had forgotten to switch it off.

There was an awkward silence as the rest of the cast assembled on stage for the photo-call, waiting for the leading lady to make her appearance. In due course, she breezed on, looking radiant, a large smile on her face, greeting everyone on stage.

'Just before we begin I must tell you a funny story,' she said, addressing me. 'I was on stage one night and I slipped. "Oh shit!" I said and thought no more about it until I returned to my dressing-room. My dresser greeted me.

"Miss, you shouldn't use language like that on stage."

"How did you know?" I asked her.

"The mikes are on," she told me!'

She paused in her narration and swept a look like a lighthouse beacon right round the auditorium, until her gaze alighted on Genista, sitting frozen on her stool. It hesitated for the slightest fraction of a second before it completed the full circle. 'Right!' she said brightly. 'Shall we start?'

Out of the corner of my eye I saw a white-faced little girl, her fists clenched and lips pressed together. It was a despairing look that turned to anguish as she dropped her head onto the white knuckles that now pressed into her eyes, to hold back the tears that threatened to engulf her . . . Curtain, blackout. And it was a blackout, as I was later to learn.

The photo-call went along without any other hitches and nothing more was said regarding the microphones.

Fifteen years or so after the incident, I happened to be once again in London on an assignment from Australia when I bumped into an actress friend. 'Funny thing,' she said, 'we were only talking about you the other day.'

'Who's "we"?' I wanted to know.

'Genista,' she replied. 'You remember Genista, don't you?'

'Course I do.'

'I'll arrange a dinner with some old mates, how about it?'

'Fantastic!' I said.

It was duly arranged and when I turned up, I was greeted by a group of old friends I hadn't seen for years, bringing back a lot of old memories.

During dinner, Genista said how much she missed working with me. She now had her own PRO business but lamented the passing of the old school of theatre photographers. Things weren't quite the same as the old days.

'Talking of the old days,' I said, 'do you remember your first photo-call?' She looked puzzled. 'The one I took you to . . . with Margaret Leighton?' She still looked puzzled, so I prompted her. 'Remember? "The mikes are on!" '

'Oh my God!' she gasped, as the memory flooded back. She visibly sagged. 'I had forgotten completely about that.'

Evidently the incident had been so traumatic that she had wiped it from her mind.

I wish that I had that capacity with some of my less pleasant memories. Some of the more agreeable happenings in my life quite often get softened with a rosy aura but the awful ones are always on total recall in sharp focus.

the 'disestablishment'...

The beginning of The Establishment's third year of existence witnessed a cooling of the public's fervour. Many memberships were not renewed. Most had achieved the purpose of their initial subscription. They had been, and been seen. As well, a lot of the late acts which were introduced, could not compete with some of the earlier coups, like Annie Ross, and the Chicago satire team, 'Second City', to name but two.

The original cast no longer appeared. Eleanor Bron was making her presence felt in 'That Was The Week That Was'. Nick Luard's magazine *Scene*, an offshoot of the club, with quality of content but not quantity of remuneration, had eaten into the kitty.

The Establishment cut its losses and sold out to a certain Mr Raymond Nash, an outcome that was to prove fatal to the already ailing club. Nash thought that the purchase of the club would automatically give him entrée into the ranks of high society, many of whom made up the membership. He was also under the misguided notion that the existing membership would continue with him, unchanged, but the underworld aura that clung to Nash further exacerbated the downward trend.

During the first week of the new ownership I was visited by a gentleman, knocking lightly on my studio door. He politely requested if he could come in. Of medium height, his stocky figure at first seemed rather flaccid, but on closer inspection, his well-cut suit revealed muscle, rather than flab. The quiet voice matched the clothes. I knew who he was and the knowledge prepared me for my reaction to his visit.

'May I come in? I'm Raymond Nash... the new owner of the club.' His smile revealed a set of perfect teeth and he looked like a successful businessman, which no doubt he was, rather than the villain which he was reputed to be. He held out his hand. 'And your new landlord,' he added with a low chuckle.

I shook his proffered hand. Someone had been shadowing him and now he came forward and introduced himself. 'Speedy!' His handshake was quite unlike Nash's firm grasp. He slid his soft hand quickly in and out, the encounter, like his eyes, furtive, as though wanting to avoid any physical or mental contact.

Nash came straight to the point. The club would be run as before. If I wished to stay, my rent would remain the same and I should continue photographing the new shows that had been booked. To all intents and purposes there would be no change. But there was. It was a change in atmosphere. No longer the buzz of excitement, the certainty of a good time, the expectancy of a chance meeting with some celebrity who was bound to be there on any given night. One's expectations were now tinged with uncertainty and tainted with the slightest hint of an unseen menace. Fewer and fewer celebrities visited the club.

Sean Kenny had been subjected to a similar visit but the outcome was quite different to mine, as I was to learn later from Speedy, who paid me a visit in the truest underworld manner. Speedy related the circumstances to me in a sort of Lebanese-American accent. 'Raymond don't like Sean, but not to worry. Raymond like you. You're OK.'

It seemed I was OK with Speedy too. He punched me lightly on the chest and said, 'OK I look after everything.' Then he patted his breast pocket and gave a conspiratorial smile. Seeing my puzzled expression he repeated the gesture, but it was manifestly clear from my lack of reaction that I had not received the message. He sidled up to me, slid his hand under his jacket and brought out an automatic pistol from the inner breast pocket. Looking at me now, he narrowed his eyes and gave a slow, knowing wink. Then he replaced the gun, nudged my ribs with his elbow and sauntered out of the studio, while I stood riveted to the floor. My throat was dry and only a faint croak emerged in reply to his 'See you later'. I managed to raise my arm mid-level and opened and closed my hand to perform a completely uncoordinated, palsied sort of '*Ciao*!'

Speedy was Nash's bodyguard and it would seem that he had appointed himself mine as well. I was 'OK'. Sean had taken objection to their visit and told them to piss off, whereupon he was given his marching orders. He managed to find a new studio space in a building next to Foyles bookshop only a few minutes away from The Establishment, which enabled me to continue my photography for him without too much inconvenience to either of us.

The Establishment lingered on for a couple of more years but the disease was terminal. Side-effects from extra-mural activities like gold smuggling and sundry criminal affairs hastened its demise. The *coup de grâce* was administered when Nash himself was arrested in Japan.

The club passed into other hands. It was sold, lock, stock and barrel to a Mr Jones, who turned it into a private 'club', by which time 17 Greek Street had turned full circle. I shifted my studio, taking over the upper floors and attic of a wonderful old paint shop housed in an eighteenth-century building, virtually next door to the now defunct Establishment. The final curtain had come down on an empty house. Adieu.

And goodbye to the shades of the entertainers who had appeared there. Those I had photographed for the noticeboard, announcing their presence at the entrance of the club included: Barry Humphries, Annie Ross, Eleanor Bron, John Bird, Jonathon Routh, Dominic Behan, John Junkin, John Antrobus, George McBeth. Just a few of the names who trod the miniscule stage in the doll's house theatre, whose dimensions belied the size of the reputation it acquired in a space of time shorter than the distance from the performers to the front-row audience.

The 40-foot illuminated sign outside 17 Greek Street no longer flashes but the legend survives, lighting up the memories of those who were fortunate enough to be there in its heyday.

don's party...

His name wasn't Don, although he threw a lot of parties. He was a don at one of the red brick universities whose mundane facades belied their contents.

There was, and still is, a lot of snobbery regarding the type of university that one attended, location being a prime factor. Oxford and Cambridge were the compulsory passwords to many a top job but the word university, proceded by a county name would bring a slight curl of the lip—especially to those people who had never attended any form of education beyond kindergarten.

Although I am not one of these, I must admit to a certain prejudice regarding Timothy, the don in question. He was the antithesis of the stereotyped don, gowned and stooped, studying the cobblestones as he hurried to his lecture, clutching his books in one hand and holding down his mortar board with the other.

Timothy would saunter to classes, head held high, his sweeping gaze searching out the pretty females in the faculty, or the younger and prettier students who happened to cross his field of vision. He set many a heart fluttering as eyes met and locked, mesmerised by his dark, long-lashed, almost feminine orbs. Quick as a blink they would find themselves attending one of his legendary parties.

The parties were pretty wild affairs, affairs being the operative word. Why students weren't sent down, or Timothy sacked, or at least admonished by those in power, can only be explained by the fact that too many in the know had also partaken of his largesse. One could always pick out the haggard participants the next day, all except for Timothy who was as disgustingly rude and healthy in the morning as he had been throughout the night.

I was invited to one of his soirées, held in the large luxurious flat that he rented. He preferred to live 'out', rather than 'in' the more restrictive confines of the university dwellings. I arrived late and the party was in full swing. That is, a lot of people busy doing their own thing, dancing to an over-amplified Rolling Stones LP. The sound was high but the lights were low as they munched on the canapés and cheese straws, drinking from glasses, tea cups and mugs, or straight from the bottle.

Forsaking the physical refreshments, I took in the visual and aural abundance that spilled from this Pandora's box. No doubt Timothy could, by dawn's early light, get all the bits and pieces back in. I broke through the sound barrier to be confronted by an undulating wall, serving as a screen for a filmic orgy that was in full swing, in glorious black and white. It had not by that time reached the dizzy heights of full colour although the positions depicted were dizzyingly colourful.

I saw a few friends sprawled on their bellies, puffing on badly rolled joints, watching the film with obvious boredom. As I sat down between them, Sally, who was on my left, rolled over and said 'hi'. Her companion also came to life.

'Hooray, a 3-D cock!' she cried, and started to unzip my jeans.

'Behave yourself,' I protested, forcibly removing her hand.

'Oh shit,' said Anne, 'it's been so boring! This is the third film we've seen and they're all alike. Fuck, suck, yuck!'

'Who brought them?' I asked.

'That creep over there,' indicated Sally. I turned and saw a very respectable, middle-aged gentleman in a three-piece suit, complete with stiff collar and tie. He was in charge of the projector, noisily whirring away.

It transpired that this bank manager-like figure, in charge of the entertainment, was a distinguished representative of the police force, and a very intimate, and I mean intimate, friend of Timothy's. I knew that Timothy was not averse to the embraces of a Wren or a Seaman, rank immaterial, a WAAF or Aircraftsman, many of whom were stationed at a base, a short bicycle ride from the university. But his involvement with a member of the blue lamp mob was something of a complete surprise.

This stalwart had brought the films and the projector, confiscated from a seedy Soho club owner awaiting trial. They were part of the evidence, as was the large block of marijuana which was rapidly diminishing, like an iceberg that had strayed into the Persian Gulf. No doubt the Soho club owner would be charged and the films returned to their appropriate place in the morning, exhibited as proof of his misdemeanours. The pot pushers would, no doubt, be released due to lack of evidence.

My gaze returned to the wall where I continued to watch the surreal spectacle of a very pale William Morris wallpaper of ornate flowers, blossoming on some rampant male organ.

making a hash of things...

Although a very heavy smoker during the rather hectic years of that decade—up to 60 a day—it was the straight variety that I inhaled. I'd tried a few puffs of the weed but was unimpressed and not inclined to further indulgence. Soon I gave up even the practice of pretending to share a joint so as not to offend my host. I recall on one occasion a rather spaced-out hop-head complaining to Miranda, 'Why do you invite Morley to your parties? He doesn't turn on, he doesn't smoke!'

'He doesn't have to smoke,' Miranda replied, 'he's turned on all the time!'

It was an admonishment which shut him up and endeared her to me, an observation brought about by the frenetic behaviour which was a normal part of my, then, lifestyle. I seemed to be on a perpetual high.

life's a drag...

The cigarette was an obvious prop in the 1920s and by the 1930s, the fairer sex had adopted it as an accessory to complement their make-up and hairstyle. Just as the fag had become a signpost of an exclusive class of English education, its namesake had become an integral part of every social class, educated or otherwise.

That the cigarette can become an extension of one's fantasy, I can vouch for through personal application. During my art school period I had returned from my first Italian trip impressed enough to have a black corduroy suit made for myself. I remember thinking that what was needed was a cigarette to round off the aura of mystery and, of course, the only suitable one to my mind, was a Black Russian Sobrani, to match my suit, my black shirt and my carefully styled black hair. It was a short-lived affectation as my grant did not really stretch beyond the necessities of food, lodgings and art materials.

Vanity, what stupidities are committed in your name! Thank God the fashion of waving a cigarette-holder had died out. What a sight I would have been, poncing around in my black suit, inserting gold-tipped Black Russians into the end of a long, no doubt, black holder—the poor man's Noel Coward, without the talent.

Smoking by the sixties had become an entrenched part of social behaviour and 'smoking' often meant more than just the lighting of a straight fag, with a Ronson or a Swan. The simple operation of smoking could now mean the dissecting of the carcass to impregnate it with 'Mary Jane', the resulting tube to be distributed among the Tom, Dick, Harry and Harriettes of the inner circle.

It could be said with some truth that a lot of artistic achievements in the sixties—music, painting and related pastimes, including sex—were joint efforts. For some, a cigarette was even *de rigueur* when taking a portrait.

Some found it a handy prop . . . what to do with their hands? Some thought it was a sign of sophistication. Some needed the calming effect of inhaling and exhaling the smoke, which soon filled the room and dispensed with the need for a soft lens.

How it was held revealed so much of the holder's character. Working-class smokers more often than not would hold the cigarette with the thumb and forefinger, thus hiding most of the hand and fingernails when taking a drag. Thus the digits and the none too perfectly manicured nails were less obvious to the viewer.

Some would hold the cigarette in a cupped hand with the lit end facing the palm so it would be totally hidden from view . . . the legacy of a quick forbidden smoko. Laid-back upper class types would make a feature of the fingers, holding the cigarette between the two top joints of the index and middle fingers, languidly moving the hand to and fro in time with their even more languid utterances.

Others would use the cigarette to emphasise a point, while the more neurotic would hold the cigarette in the crutch of the first two fingers, so the thumb would obscure part of the face when they too had a drag. In this instance it became a mask to hide behind.

The unlit cigarette became an object to allay anxiety, a talisman to ward off bad vibes by studying it closely and thus avoiding eye contact. Passing it from hand to hand made it a sort of 'lay' rosary, a singular worry bead.

The exhibitionist satisfied his desires for attention by shouting, 'OOOh, look at me', spelt out with a series of perfectly executed 'ooos' in the form of smoke rings.

Finally, there is the oral junkie. Someone who must have something in their mouth. Me.

My first cigarette of the day, and I say it with a modicum of pride, was not until I had finished breakfast. There, the restraint ended. It was one continual ritual of taking a cigarette from the packet, tapping it, to pack the tobacco tighter, lighting up and puffing away, then snuffing out the stub and starting all over again.

This continued throughout the day and if, for some reason, I was caught without a cigarette when the telephone rang, I couldn't answer it until I had lit up. If I had run out, my secretary would pull out one of her cigarettes, put it in my mouth, strike a match to light it and hand me the phone, all in one perfect gesture. Practice makes perfect.

I used cigarettes as a screen to separate me from the realities I wished to avoid, and there were all the little things I could indulge in without the ritual, to sidestep, or at least delay, issues which had to be faced.

Looking through my negatives I am astounded by the percentage of the sitters clutching, flaunting, hiding, lighting, or dangling these coffin nails as appendages to their personalities during the 1960s. These many years on we have the anti-smoking lobby to thank, saving us from having to eat in a haze of smoke, or look at films through a grey fog. Travelling on buses or trains now no longer means leaving the conveyance smelling like a kipper.

No doubt you must be aware that I have given up the noxious habit of smoking and there is nothing more obnoxious, more virtuous, than a reformed whore.

Imogene Hassall and Charlotte Rampling...

I was lying awake in my bed in a Paris hotel, for some reason, unable to sleep. Although the hotel was on the corner of La Place de la Concorde, it was very quiet. The incessant honking of horns and screeching of tyres as accelerators or brakes were applied with lead-filled shoes, was absent. The streams of cars and taxies that pour into that 'Place de la Discord', frantically searching for an exit to the Champs Elysées, had not yet reassembled from the previous night's retreat. It was three in the morning.

I switched on the bedside radio which had been left on an English-speaking station. It was a news program when I wanted some soothing music. As I sleepily groped to switch stations, my hand was halted inches from the dial when I heard the name Imogene Hassall mentioned. My interest turned to disbelief when it was followed by the horrific statement '... was found dead...' followed by an impersonal description of pills found at her side. How? Why?

How was easily determined—the ever-popular solution, sleeping tablets. Why, was a much harder question to answer. The only person who could supply the true reason was, of course, the instigator and that answer could no longer be revealed. The deed, hiding the motive, hiding the deed.

When I first met her, Imogene was a very attractive young actress who had been sent to me by her agent for a portrait sitting. She was petite but her lack of inches were fully compensated for by a liberal dash of exoticism. I always called her 'the dusky maid'.

During that first session as I looked at her features through the viewfinder, I remarked how alike she was to Vivien Leigh.

'So we should be,' she said, tossing her head to flick back the hair falling across her beautiful eyes. 'We've both got Indian blood.'

'I didn't know that,' I exclaimed in surprise, 'but now that you've told me, I can see the Ganges trickling through your veins... but it can't match the Whampoa waters coursing through mine!'

I explained that I was half-Chinese and therefore that my percentage was stronger than the solution she was flaunting.

'Yes, there are quite a few of us in the business who aren't too keen on the knowledge being shared,' she continued. 'Merle Oberon, Cliff Richard...' and she went on to name other names. It was like a freemasons' lodge where the bloodlines are known only to those who shared the common stream.

'From now on,' I said, 'you'll always be the dusky maid,' and we laughed, sharing the joke as we shared the knowledge of our mixed antecedents which gave extra bonding to our friendship.

Another bit of sharing was a much more tenuous link. John Hassall, of 'Skegness is so bracing' poster fame was her grandfather and I had in my possession a large pastel drawing of a cavalier by him. When she saw it, she wanted it very much and offered to buy it. I, of course, wanted to keep it and had to refuse her. Quite often when we met the opening greeting would be, 'Still got the Hassall?' and on these occasions we would part with Imogene's 'See you! Sure you don't want to sell it?'

We didn't see each other all that often, sometimes at parties, first nights or the odd visit to my studio. I photographed a play in the West End, *Afternoon Men*, in which she starred with Pauline Boty, James Fox and Peter Bowles. It was based on an Anthony Powell novel. She was also in a film, *Bed Time*, written by Michael Hastings, in which there was a controversial nude scene which I think was edited in the final cut.

Imogene's legacy of images lie in my archives, many of them actually printed for the first time to help write this chapter of her short life. Another part of the legacy were the early photographs of her friend, Charlotte Rampling.

Charlotte had seen the results of Imogene's first sitting and was impressed enough to ask her to arrange a similar session for herself. I must admit that the sequence of sessions I had with Charlotte are, like my filing system, quite jumbled.

She arrived at my studio for her portrait with her companion, Jeremy Lloyd, whom, if I recall correctly, had also come for his portrait. The results were that in between the two sessions I took a roll of them larking about. The main interest for me in these particular photographs now, thirty years later, is her hairstyle, which was classic late 1960s, a long mop, with back-combing at the crown to give it height.

At another time I did a series of very casual and candid pictures of her, relaxing at her digs. Some time later, Charlotte asked me to take some fashion photographs to make into a composite, so she could try fashion work. She didn't need to pursue this sideline because within a short time she was once more in front of my camera, but this time as an established star, modelling a fashion page in a magazine for which I freelanced.

How do some actors make it while others don't? Talent? Charisma? And why do some catch the public's fancy, while others, perhaps more dedicated and talented, will never attain star status, but will give stunning performances in supporting roles for the rest of their lives?

Why are some more able to bend with the stresses of life while others snap and how is it that one, when confronted by failure will give in, while the other will face adversity and win?

How and why, I don't know. All I know is that one of the little stars in my part of the sky stopped twinkling and another grew brighter and brighter and is still gaining in intensity.

the bare facts... Pauline Boty...

'You photographed my wife in the nude!'

'I've photographed a lot of wives in the nude,' I replied flippantly, to cover my annoyance and feeling of unease. Who the hell was his wife? Before I had a chance to ask he spoke again.

'She's dead you know,' and his drink slurped over the rim of the glass, held by an unsteady hand.

'Who?' I yelled above the din of the party, which I wasn't enjoying, even before his intrusion. Panic had seized me by now. What had I to do with his wife's death?

'Pauline,' he said.

'What Pauline?' I asked, my mind trying desperately to remember.

'Pauline Boty,' he choked. Emotion overtook him and turning his back on me, he lurched across the room, spilling a few other drinks in his progress.

My companion gave me a long, questioning look. I shrugged my shoulders. 'I'm going,' I said, and left without further explanation. As I drove home I tried to sort out what had led up to this evening's confrontation.

Several years before I had paid a visit to the Royal College of Art where several of my fellow art students were engaged in further study, after their initial training at Twickenham Art School. I had, by this time, given up any serious attempt at earning my living as an artist and I was freelancing as a photographer.

Someone, somewhere, had decided that Pauline Boty, a student of stained glass at the college who was also the chairman of the Anti-Ugly League, a student organisation protesting against anything that was not aesthetically pleasing, should be photographed for an article to publicise the league. Under the circumstances, it was natural that I was elected to take the photograph.

I took several photographs of her that day, showing a blonde, vivacious girl, filled with *joie de vivre* but there was no indication of the disease that would end her life, tragically early. She was stunning, a major factor in why the article found a place in the William Hickey column of the *Daily Express.*

During the intervening years I photographed Pauline for various reasons—portraits for her agent, when she became involved in acting, fashion photography where I used her as a model in her studio and portraits just for herself. Then there were front-of-house pictures for the play, *Afternoon Men*, and of course, the nudes which had caused such an outburst from her husband.

One of the prestige glossy magazines had commissioned me to find four beautiful theatrical ladies, for a colour spread in a forthcoming issue. They were to be tasteful pin-ups, the amount of body covering left to my discretion.

I received the assignment while working on another article, which rejoiced in the title of 'Do-It-Yourself Furniture with the Stars'. I had finished with Morecambe and Wise and was now photographing Michael Caine at home, with his little homemade bookcase. I voiced my dilemma. How to find nice young ladies who were willing to bare a little bit of flesh for the sake of art and a model's fee?

'Phone Edina Ronay,' he said. 'Tell her what you want and tell her I said it was all right.'

Next I approached Tsai Chin of *The World of Suzie Wong* fame and with a little arm twisting—a mental Chinese burn—and a lot of pleading, in both English and Chinese, she agreed.

The photographs of these two ladies were very discreet and when I came to photograph Pauline, I showed her the photographs I had taken. Over coffee, I broached the subject of clothing. She regarded me with a wicked grin and said she didn't think she had anything really suitable for these pictures. Then a brainwave struck her and she leapt up and rushed out of the room slamming the door behind her. Before I realised what was happening, the door was flung open and there stood Pauline.

'Perfect!' she said.

Standing before me was this Junoesque figure, stark naked, but for a large smile and a bunch of paper flowers, delicately held in one hand that covered the strategic area of her well-rounded hips.

We took it from there and tried other strategic coverings, with cushions and paintings substituting for flowers. We had great fun doing the shots, both in colour and black and white. It was, and still remains, the most enjoyable and relaxed nude session I ever photographed.

Before I had the opportunity to photograph the fourth model I was informed by the editor that the project had been spiked.

I gave a set of contacts to Pauline so she could choose some black and white blow-ups for herself, and showed her the colour transparencies.

Some time later she married and was just emerging as a successful actress when she was diagnosed as having leukaemia. When Pauline died, the artist Derick Boshier asked for the loan of the transparencies from the session to use as part of a memorial tribute to Pauline. Peter Blake, I believe, was to assist in getting it together.

I eventually got my transparencies back but I never saw any evidence of the intended tribute. Perhaps there were objections from those close to her, or perhaps they just never got around to it, and I never discovered what her husband had wanted to convey to me when he accosted me at that party.

FASHION DEVOTEES

Sixties fashion, to a degree, passed me by. I generally wore the uniform of the photographer, black leather jacket and jeans, although I did have a pink suede leather suit which I wore with a black polo-neck sweater. At art school it was pink shirts with black corduroy trousers and Black Sobrani cigarettes, but the nearest I got to Mod, as in Mods and Rockers, was when I was married. I wore an Edwardian suit made up by Connock & Lockie, who were very up-market tailors. I didn't go so far as to have velvet lapels but I did have cloth-covered buttons. I'd switch from jeans to the Edwardian suit and that was about as outrageous as I got.

There was a phase when I wore Black Watch tartan trousers which one could get quite cheap from the Army Surplus stores. They were very nicely made and came up high to hug the waist. But I was not a devotee of fashion and believe me, fashion is a religion.

the hierarchies...

The early fashion photographers were all a little bit upper-crust and the models were a little bit that way too. Then the sixties came with its working-class boy photographers and a whole lot of little scrubbers who became models... dolly birds.

One still found the elegant girls working in *haute couture* who couldn't do the mini skirts and so on, but it was the working-class girls who looked best in the Carnaby Street stuff. And if the *haute couture* is High Church, then the little scrubbers go to a Baptist Chapel. But they still got caught up in it, spending their last cent on something which was fashionable, not Dior, or St Laurent, but Polly Peck, or who-ever the mass market designer was.

Carnaby Street was tacky, glitzy fashion, full of mini skirts and fake everything—fake fur, fake leather, fake suede, fake velvet. It was raucous and ostentatious, almost a five and ten cent store. For a bit more class one went to the Kings Road, Chelsea where there were some good boutiques and occasionally one saw some celebrity. In Carnaby Street it was all the little girls who screamed at the Beatles. I did quite a lot of fashion shots down there for John Fenton, which was a middling fashion house of the period.

Carnaby Street was five minutes from my studio and filled with Japanese tourists and lots of Germans, all looking for 'swinging London'. But it wasn't there. If it was anywhere it was at private parties, where being abandoned was expected and shedding one's gear was equated with shedding one's inhibitions.

two novitiates... Jean Shrimpton and Twiggy...

I did other fashion work for people like John Anstey and for fashion features for magazines like *GO*. This was a new travel magazine, the latest addition to the privileged family of publications headed by *Queen*.

Anstey had seen my work and phoned to arrange a meeting. At that time I was engaged in a lot of reportage articles for *The Tatler* and various women's magazines, with the occasional newspaper shot thrown in. Anstey told me that he wanted me to photograph a fashion feature but he didn't want me to be a 'fashion photographer'. 'Keep to your style of reportage photography,' he told me. 'I want casual pictures, not high fashion.' It seemed to work because I was asked to repeat the format with him on another occasion, with Susannah York, in Paris.

On this occasion the location was the racetrack at Newmarket. Anstey picked me up from my studio and I squeezed into the back seat of his car, next to the male model, a mature, very British gent with a bowler hat on his head and a tightly rolled umbrella between his knees. On the other side sat a very quiet girl with vestiges of puppy fat still evident. She said nothing until we arrived at the racetrack where we were to shoot.

'I'm a little nervous,' she confessed. 'It's my first job.'

'Me too,' I replied. It was my first big fashion job. I'd done the odd 'hat' shot and photographs for newspapers, but this was my first 'glossy'.

In the hurried trip from Soho to the location, Anstey, who was an ex-racing car driver, had failed to introduce us. Now I asked her name. 'Jean,' she replied, 'Jean Shrimpton.'

It was a very easy session in spite of my first night nerves. She was a natural with none of the stiffness that one usually encounters with novitiates. The only sour note was that she had to use the ladies loo as a dressing room. It was a very primitive introduction to the high-powered stage that she was to step onto within a very short period of time.

The photos were published in a five-page feature, leading off with a double-page spread. They were her first published pictures and as it turned out, the only time I ever photographed her. Later, I tried to book her for another job but was informed by the agency that she was unavailable. She was working for *Vogue*, or more to the point, David Bailey.

I was introduced to Bailey one evening in The Establishment's jazz cellar, situated three floors below my studio. The cellar was, as usual, very crowded. Dudley Moore, as usual, was at the piano and I, as usual, if I happened to be working late and had a little time to spare between commitments, could be found sipping a coke and listening to the jazz.

I literally bumped into Jean, sandwiched between two males. One was a dapper, slim, elegantly dressed person, Mark Boxer, while the other was an amply fleshed-out, not too smartly attired youth. 'I see you've lost some weight Lewis,' said Mark, being a little bitchy. I had, much to my dismay, put on as many pounds as I had spent on too many visits to La Maison Berteaux where I overdosed on *café au lait* and their wonderful French pastries.

Seeing that Mark and I were already familiar, Jean introduced me to her other escort, who stood, silently regarding the scene with a glower. 'Hi,' he said unenthusiastically.

'Hi,' I rejoined with equal fervour. We didn't even shake hands. This was my first and last close encounter with Bailey.

The only other sighting was during a private, up-market debutante fashion show, where he turned up as a spectator with his newly acquired wife, Catherine Deneuve. They were seated about fifteen feet away. I swung my camera away from the mannequins I was photographing and because of the distance separating us, flashed one hopeful exposure before returning to the job at hand.

'I'm her manager'...

'Look! There's one,' said Theo Goldrey, excitedly pointing at a figure carrying an untidily wrapped brown paper parcel, crisscrossed with string.

Theo wasn't interested in the parcel. It was the shaggy fur coat engulfing the slim figure that had caught her attention. We were working on a fashion feature entitled 'Fashion in the Streets' for the magazine, *London Life*. This entailed finding people wearing clothes which were clearly not the creation of any fashion house, but which were nevertheless unusual enough to be fashionable, rather than just bizarre. I ran across and stopped her.

'Excuse me, we're doing a fashion feature,' pointing to Theo, dodging cars as she crossed the road, following me. 'Can I take your pho——'. Before I had time to finish my request a tall, saturnine young man wearing a dark, double-breasted suit interposed himself between the camera and the fur coat. Any aura of mystery that should have surrounded him was dispelled by the casualness of his shirt, worn open at the collar, bereft of a tie.

'Can I help you?' he demanded with just a hint of aggressive cockiness, making the question rather different from the same request at Harrod's. I explained what we were after and immediately his demeanour changed and he became very cooperative.

'Who are you?' I wanted to know.

'I'm her manager.'

'Her manager?' I queried.

'Yes, she's a model and I'm her manager,' he repeated.

'What's her name?'

'Twiggy.'

'Twiggy who?'

'Twiggy! . . . just Twiggy.'

Other information followed at a more leisurely pace, allowing Theo to put in her notes that the manager's name was Justin de Villeneuve. He was grooming Twiggy, who had given up her job as a hairdresser's assistant to be a fashion model. The fur coat had been bought for five pounds in Portobello market.

Twiggy's long legs were encased in patterned knitted stockings, her feet in low-heeled, strapped, 'grandma' pumps of black leather, matching the handbag dangling from its strap in her left hand. She was nicknamed Twiggy because of her body's stick-like appearance. It was to be her professional name and it stuck, along with the Cockney accent, throughout her career.

The name caught the public's imagination, fuelled by a press that latched onto its uniqueness. They exploited it relentlessly as she rocketed to early fame, first as a model and then as a pop star, stage star, film star and celebrity interviewee. It wasn't until many years after her initial success that the public was let into the secret that her real name was Lesley Hornby.

The picture of Twiggy and her manager appeared in the article and was her first published photo. I have been responsible for taking the first published pictures of each of three, internationally acclaimed models, Jean Shrimpton, Twiggy and Maggie Eckhardt, but I cannot take any credit for 'discovering' them. They were literally put in front of my camera by fate and I just pressed the shutter.

Justin de Villeneuve was the first of the middle men I met, who in time came to secure celebrity status themselves; the Svengalis, the pushers. In the old days people had done their own dirty work, without an agent but now the age of the entrepreneur appeared to have arrived.

Their work was to elevate attractive but otherwise unexceptional people into stars, products of publicity. All that was needed was for someone to grab it and publicise it, even negative publicity would do it. If one became notorious, one became wanted.

Admittedly the person in question had to have some form of charisma, to exude a certain something which could be built up, and up, and up.

when you and I were young Maggie Eckhardt…

Felicity Green, the fashion editor of the *Daily Mirror*, phoned to let me know she'd be sending around a hat to be photographed. She was using a new model who had recently arrived from Australia, whose name was Maggie Eckhardt. She had worked for Norman Hartnell as a mannequin during one of his visits to Australia, and he was impressed enough to advise her to leave Australia to work in London.

The hat to be photographed had arrived the day before the shoot and Maggie was booked for 11 am. At about 10.30, a tall, trousered, leggy girl, dressed in a heavy knit, Arran-type sweater peered around the studio door, after a hesitant knock. She squinted through a pair of large glasses with heavy black frames, perched on her nose under a rat's nest of black dishevelled hair. *Oh Lor*, I thought to myself. Another hopeful looking for a job or some test shots.

I asked her in and offered her a cup of coffee which she eagerly accepted. We passed a few other pleasantries concerning the weather and other forgettable topics but she did not broach the subject of wanting some test shots. I was similarly quiet, not wanting to get involved with more non-essential work.

She declined the extra cup of coffee so I glanced obviously at my watch, hoping she would take the hint and leave, so I could get on with some last minute adjustments to the lighting set-up. Then I murmured something about models being late.

'Are you expecting another model?' she asked.

'Yes,' I replied with mounting irritation. 'She should have been here at eleven... some new model called Maggie Eckhardt.'

She looked at me with utter disbelief. 'But I'm Maggie Eckhardt,' she said.

'Oh God,' I replied, 'I thought you were some bird after test shots.'

We both fell about laughing but she wasn't at all put out. I told her it was a head shot and left her to her own devices. After an absence of about fifteen minutes she reappeared, her hair drawn back as requested, each hair perfectly behaved, not one out of place. Her glasses had been removed, revealing a pair of really lustrous eyes. Her make-up was restrained for the sixties and she had removed the bulky sweater to expose a quite exquisite neck, rising from shoulders that revealed well-defined collar bones, without looking boney. It was no wonder she became one of Yves St Laurent's favourite models and was used by photographers like Michel Molinare, Claude Virgin, Richard Avedon, Art Kane, Kublin, Horvat and many others.

In keeping with Shrimpton and Twiggy, my shot from this session was also her first published photograph. Also in line with the others was the fact that it was the one and only occasion on which I used her.

summer of our malcontent... Susannah York...

We were getting the red carpet treatment, leaving for France in a chartered aircraft. There were five of us. John Anstey and his wife, Michael Wells with his, and myself. But it was Michael's wife who was getting the VIP send-off, complete with a Fleet Street photographer, one of the older school, with his four by five press camera and his flash gun. There he was, kneeling on one knee, shouting out instructions that were being carried away by the gale that was blowing across the tarmac. But Mrs Wells was reacting like the pro she was, doing what she knew was wanted without having to be told.

She climbed up to the door of the aircraft, then turned around and waved. The portly, middle-aged flasher, deluding himself that she was carrying out his implicit instructions, was beaming with satisfaction as he exposed two sheets of film in rapid succession. His dexterity exposed him as one of a vanishing breed of Fleet Street photographers. Stoic, reliable men—they were always men to my knowledge—who waited patiently in the pouring rain or blistering sun to get their shots. Some of their results may not have been dramatic but the lead-up certainly was. The mechanics of working the cumbersome equipment, transferring double dark slides from pocket to camera and back, and in between slamming in the slide, withdrawing the shield, exposing, replacing, flipping over to the other side, cocking the shutter and repeating, was drama of the highest order.

Having taken his shots he turned around to catch me in the act of photographing the photographer, photographing the model. He regarded my miniature camera with scorn and a small, pitying smile—I didn't know if the smile was for me or for himself—demonstrated that he was aware that this 'toy' was rapidly usurping the role of his grown-up camera and soon would be responsible for replacing both of them.

He took a few notes from the blonde he had just finished photographing, jotting down the answers she gave to the routine questions that all the rising young stars were asked.

Yes, *Greengage Summer* had been well received, and yes, she was excited to be going off to Paris to do a fashion feature. Twenty minutes later, all baggage stowed and formalities attended to, we took off. I was seated next to Michael's wife, the blonde model, off to Paris to do her fashion feature. She was Susannah York.

It was an uneventful flight to Le Touquet. There, we all squeezed into the car that John Anstey was driving to our Paris rendezvous. No sooner had Anstey put his foot on the accelerator than our troubles began. It was the start of a series of minor happenings and irritations that built up with explosive force by the end of the assignment.

We roared down the tree-lined road leading to Paris, with Susie seated between Mike and myself, clutching her husband's hand so tightly that her knuckles gleamed white. Worried murmurings passed between them. I wasn't perturbed, having driven with Anstey before and knowing that as a former racing car driver, he was fully in control. I quietly imparted this fact to Susie who fell silent, still clutching Mike's hand. Minutes later an explosive bang hit the car, accompanied by a piercing scream from Susie as the car screeched to a halt. There was a deafening silence punctuated by low sobs from Susie. The rest of us were paralysed by the unexpected impact. Anstey unstrapped himself and got out to inspect the windscreen which was now partly obscured by feathers and blood. A large bird had flown into us and wiped itself out. Anstey calmly wiped the screen clear, returned to his seat and dismissed the whole incident. 'It was only a pigeon.'

The rest of the journey was completed in silence until Susie, Mike and myself were dropped off at our hotel, while the Ansteys continued on to theirs. Our puzzlement turned to resentment when it was discovered that although we had been booked into a luxury hotel, John and his wife had ensconced themselves in a super-luxury one. Susie felt slighted and started to regret coming. Mike had come, all expenses paid, on the understanding that he would model a dinner jacket with Susie in her evening dress.

The night before we were due to start work we were dining in the hotel restaurant and the resentment of the earlier incidents had given way to a more mellow mood. Susie had asked me to give them a knock on the way down to the dining room and this I did. There was no response for a moment, then a hesitant, 'Who is it?'

'It's Lewis.'

'Oh, . . . OK. Hold on for a moment. I'm coming.' More scuffling and hurried whispers then Susie opened the door with a giggle while Mike sat on the edge of the dishevelled bed, a coy smile on his flushed face. I had obviously arrived a littel too early. We made our way down to the dining room, they more relaxed than they had been all day.

The next morning, after breakfast, we made our way to the Ansteys' hotel, only a stone's-throw from ours, and were greeted with the news that John wasn't feeling too well. We would have to start the session without him. Luckily I knew Paris and found locations without wasting time. I had attended the Académie La Grande Chaumière for life-classes, so fortunately there were no complications when I used one of the studios as a location.

We crossed Paris by foot, Metro and car, happily snapping away, changing dresses with each location . . . the flower market, Sacré Coeur, the flea market, Montparnasse and Montmartre and lots of doorways and little streets in between.

It was a happy two days shooting but on the third day things started to sour. It was late afternoon and Mike should have started preparing for the evening's shot. Suddenly he decided that he didn't want to model the clothes, saying that he wasn't really wanted, was only there because he was Susannah York's husband.

Mike was also an actor and an image problem may have played a large part in his reluctance to cooperate. Susie was annoyed and let her feelings show. Mike walked off in a huff and I was left without a male model. I wasn't familiar with the French model agencies and to arrange a casting session at this late hour would have been impossible. Then a possible solution struck me.

A few months earlier I had been in Paris on a fashion assignment, photographing some knitwear with an English model, Sally Greenhill. I had been shooting by the statue of Joan of Arc in the Rue de Rivoli when a young man caught my eye, indicating that he knew me with a smile and jerk of the head. When I finished the roll he approached me. 'I don't know if you remember me. My name is Love and I was at the same art school as you, but I was one of the juniors.'

Lewis Morley and the Fringe boys.

Peter Cook.

The Fringe cast (*from left to right*):
Jonathon Miller, Peter Cook, Dudley Moore and Alan Bennett.

John Cleese and Connie Booth (*top*).
Charlotte Rampling and Jeremy Lloyd (*bottom*).

The Establishment cast (*from left to right*):
John Fortune, Eleanor Bron, Geremy Geidt and John Bird.

David Hamilton (*top*). Susannah York and Michael Wells (*bottom*).

Pauline Boty.

Lindsay Anderson (*left*).

Albert Finney.

John Thaw (*top*) and Donald Sutherland (*bottom*).

Johnny Speight.

David Frost.

Christine Keeler.

Michael Caine.

Marsha Hunt.

Clint Eastwood.

I couldn't recall the face but the name was familiar because there had been another junior by the name of Kiss, and Kiss and Love were the best of friends. He told me he was now working in Paris as a graphic designer, and was sharing digs with the art director of *Elle*, the French fashion magazine.

The art director also turned out to be English and over coffee that evening I found out his name, David Hamilton. He later became better known as a photographer of young girls in misty situations. It had been a pleasant evening, well spent as it stood me in good stead that day in Paris when Mike did a bunk.

I rushed into a nearby cafe, bought a jeton and looked up the number of *Elle*. As luck would have it David Hamilton was still there and I breathlessly told him of my predicament. Could he get me a model?

'It's a bit late Lewis,' he replied. 'If you'd contacted me earlier this afternoon, I could have helped.'

Grasping at straws, I blurted out, 'How about you? You're about the same size as the model, couldn't you step in and take his place?

'I'm an art director,' he replied indignantly. 'I can't be seen in my own magazine modelling!'

'Sorry David,' I said apologetically. 'I understand. Catch up with you some time.'

'Yeah,' he replied. 'See you later. Oh, by the way, just as a matter of interest, who's the female model?'

'Susannah York,' I replied.

I don't have to state the obvious but he slipped into the vacant suit quicker than anyone could say Jacques Faith. The day was saved but the negs were lost, that is, after the article was published. David wrote to me and asked if he could borrow the negs to do some prints for himself as he didn't want to put me to any trouble or expense. He would return them as soon as he was finished with them. It would seem that he still hasn't finished with them because I have never got them back.

The next morning, Susie and I went to see about the last day's shoot and to get Mrs Anstey and the clothes. Throughout all the drama we hadn't seen John who had been confined to bed. This morning, after the doctor left, he called us into his bedroom to ask how things were progressing.

'How're you feeling?' I enquired.

'Much better now,' he said. 'The doctor said I'd be fit to travel in a couple of days.'

'What was the matter?' asked Susie.

'It was nothing,' volunteered Mrs Anstey, '. . . just measles.'

I saw the horrified look on Susie's face as she stepped back, shaking her head in disbelief. She turned and hurried from the room. When I caught up with her she was livid.

'He's got measles and he didn't tell us,' she exploded. 'I've never had measles, God, I could catch it and I'm due to start a film. I've a good mind to sue him. I'm going to phone my agent, I'm going to fly back to London straightaway.'

Later she calmed down and we finished off the job at hand and the next day returned to London. The Ansteys followed separately, no charter flight this time. Nothing more was said, the article was published and that was that.

In the following years I did quite a lot of work with Susie. Various fashion shots for other magazines, stills for a short film about nuns, front-of-house photos for two plays and a couple of portrait sessions.

It was during one of these that she saw some photographs of Albert Finney which I had taken for *Billy Liar* and she said that she would love to meet him. 'Come off it Susie,' I replied. 'I'm sure you could meet him any time you wanted.'

'Don't you believe it,' she replied. 'I can't just go up to him and introduce myself.'

Finney was at that time appearing in Osborne's *Luther* at the Royal Court, which I had been wanting to see. 'Tell you what,' I suggested, 'how about going to see *Luther* and I'll take you backstage and introduce you to him?'

So it was arranged that Susie and Mike would take myself and my wife to dinner and then we would take them to the theatre. At the end of the performance as we all started to make our way towards the stage door, Mike pulled his Paris trick.

'I'm sure Albert doesn't want to meet me... I don't want...'

'Mike!' Susie pleaded, but before another drama could develop my wife, Pat, took control and settled the matter.

'I've met Albert,' she said. 'Mike, you don't want to, so how about the two of us sit and wait in the car while Susie and Lewis go?'

This took the wind out of the sails of whatever vessel he had in mind to navigate into a storm and he grudgingly followed Pat out to the car.

In his dressing room, Albert was the genial host. 'What will you have to drink?' he asked. Susie was flustered. I think coming face to face with her hero was a bit too much for her.

'What shall I have to drink?' she asked me.

'Have some white wine,' I suggested, seeing an open bottle next to an array of alcoholic beverages piled on the table.

'Have you got a cigarette?' gasped Susie. She nervously took one from my packet but before I had time to light it, Albert was back with the drinks. The next minute he was back with a packet of cigarettes, offering one to Susie.

'Thank you,' she whispered and held out her free hand, from which the crumpled cigarette I had given her fell. Albert didn't show any sign of noticing. Always the gentleman.

A few years later I was photographing Donleavy's *A Singular Man* for front-of-house, with Susie in the lead. We lunched together during the afternoon break. She had in the meantime made *Tom Jones* with Albert Finney.

'Well Susie,' I remarked. 'I expect you got to know Albert well during the shooting of the film?'

She gave me a look that gave nothing away and answered with one terse word. 'Yes!'

Nothing more was forthcoming and I took it to mean, 'Don't ask!' I didn't.

getting sidetracked...

You have to be a very good model to relax in a studio context, against a white background, but when I had my choice of using models in a natural setting, I always chose actresses.

They were better at a shooting situation, like sitting at a table or running along a beach. A professional model would have been too 'modelly' but an actress could relax in a natural background and give to the clothes a quality with which the viewer could identify. But modelling was a double-edged sword. If an actor became too successful as a model before becoming established, and the face had been extensively exposed, there was always a sneering reference from their fellow professionals when they made it in their rightful niche. The less dedicated could also be sidetracked from a too strenuous thespian pursuit when the immediate rewards from modelling became a temptation too great to resist.

It was different if a well-known actor did a bit of modelling for promotional purposes, just the odd appearance in a respectable paper or magazine. Then it was helpful all round. I had used Susannah York, Jeremy Kemp, Anna Massey, Sian Phillips, Charlotte Rampling, Jimmy Tarbuck, Jimmy Young, Billy J. Kramer and even Bobby Moore, captain of the English Soccer Team to this end.

erotic imperialism...

The feature using Pauline Boty, Edina Roney and Tsai Chin had been spiked because of a messy exchange of letters and a lot of damaging publicity concerning the cover of a recent issue of the magazine in question. It was a photo of a Caucasian lady in the embrace of a very dark-hued gentleman. Various readers had cancelled their subscriptions on the basis that they objected to a Negro embracing a white woman. Accusations of racism had been bandied about, even though the 'Negro' was in fact white, just very well-tanned. But the damage had been done and the advertisers had threatened to withdraw their patronage, meaning that nothing controversial could now be printed.

Foreign models were only starting to get a foothold in the advertising industry at this time. One could use Oriental models and even black models, provided they were female. Although a white man and a coloured girl in juxtaposition immediately suggested a sexual thing, it was acceptable because there was the unspoken implication that the white was more powerful and so could have access to a non-white sexual object. The reverse, however, of a black man with a white girl meant only one thing to many people. 'My God! He's going to screw her!'

The standards have changed now because there are so many more non-white consumers who will buy the clothes or use the products. One even sees advertisements featuring white women and black men, but I think women's lib has something to do with it. The white woman still holds the power, only now it is acceptable to many that she can exercise her rights and have a non-white sexual object. Erotic imperialism meets economic need.

pre sunset strip... Tom Jones...

With my camera at the ready, I was tucked away in the corner of Tom Jones' bedroom so as not to get in the way of what was happening. The young girl with the heavily made up eyes stood watching as the singer started to strip.

I began to photograph as he took off his shirt, revealing a smooth, well-rounded torso, a gold chain and medallion hanging on a chest that boasted only a hint of down between the nipples and scattered around the navel.

In later years, on the evidence of other photographs, this area assumed a hirsute covering that you could wipe your feet on, a feat that either sex, for differing reasons would gladly have performed.

He looked down past his navel to locate the zip on his trousers, then glancing up he saw the girl slowly approaching. He fumbled a bit but managed to unzip the fly and kicking off his shoes, he let the trousers drop around his ankles.

She knelt in front of him and placed a pair of black trousers, trimmed with a wide, patterned, black and white margin, on the floor next to his feet. Bending down, he picked them up and struggled into the tight, flare-bottoms as the girl proceeded to button on a busily patterned shirt with a Tyrolean halter to cover his nudity.

Tom Jones was trying on a collection of clothes that the girl, Sylvia Gosse, a fashion designer, had created for him.

The clothes looked bizarre and completely out of place in the suburban bedroom, with its Venetian blinds and box-springed bed. After photographing three or four of the outfits, I felt that the clothes also looked bizarre and out of place on Tom Jones, even allowing for their sixties vintage. But then I have always been a bit of a square.

After the camera and clothes had been packed away we were presented with a bit of Welsh hospitality, a welcome, if not in the valleys, at least in the front sitting room, with a cup of tea prepared by his wife.

Las Vegas was never so far away.

raisin in the fog... Marsha Hunt...

'Hi! Would you take some pictures of me?'

Somehow, there was this girl who had materialised in my studio, Cheshire cat-like. It was a very American voice, accompanied by a very large smile. More *café* than *lait*, her skin had a luminous sheen, like satinised gun metal and her hair was teased out to surround her face with a black, wire-wool halo.

I was surprised by her sudden appearance. Back in the days when my studio was situated on the first floor of The Establishment, with the tape-recorder endlessly churning out music and the forty-cup, Westinghouse coffee machine perpetually perking with coffee, it would have been unremarkable. Then, the coffee machine would be filled and emptied three times daily by thirsty clients, visitors, and other hangers-on who had wandered up uninvited, from the club below.

What with the constant washing of cups and emptying of ash trays, my secretary and assistants were glad when those days were over and life had returned to catering for a less hectic set of friends, art directors, account executives, actors and models.

The layout of the new studio was different, with the reception area now one floor above the workspace. Now here was this girl, who informed me her name was Marsha, taking me back to that chaotic time. She had ignored the notice indicating 'Reception' and had come straight into the studio itself, my sacrosanct domain.

'I'm Marsha,' she repeated, 'Marsha Hunt. I'm in *Hair*.'

No, she wasn't a wig saleswoman but a member of the cast of the American musical *Hair* which had landed on the West End stage with an impact which was shaking the packed audiences during its long run.

Hair was more than just a musical in terms of song and dance. It was a social commentary, a political and moral protest, a plea for humanity and a paean for peace, yet to come. It was a love child of that messy coupling of Vietnam and the United States, fuelled by the anti-Vietnam War sentiments that permeated the youth of the day. But that was only part of the reason for its appeal, for the older generation too flocked to the theatre, attracted perhaps by the exhibition of youthful bodies in various stages of undress, during the nightly, orchestrated invasion of the stage.

Marsha and I spent the afternoon chatting and drinking coffee, and snapping off some shots of her, both in colour and black and white. Most distinctive was her eye make-up, very sixties, more revealing than flared jeans, more accurate at freezing a point in time.

This was the time of 'flowers in your hair' and peace in your hearts, and it wasn't only confined to San Francisco.

Trafalgar Square witnessed the swelling ranks of the beatniks and peaceniks who, driven by love in their hearts and a degree of anti-American feeling, meandered under the waving red banners and protest slogans towards the quartet of lions at the foot of Nelson's column. Meanwhile Nelson perched, uninvolved, like Pilate, looking away from the American Embassy, where this multitude was soon to descend.

As the trickle made its way to Grosvenor Square, led by Tariq Ali and Vanessa Redgrave who brandished a petition to deliver to the US Ambassador, it was joined by others with differing motives, fascist sympathisers and just plain troublemakers. Shop windows were smashed *en route*, scuffles broke out among the ranks and it became clear that the police, who were having trouble keeping order, were losing their grip on the situation.

As the mass of demonstrators flooded into the Square, they were confronted by the mounted police, who had been alerted to the danger that the crowd could turn into a mob. It did, and the resulting mêlée became known as the Battle of Grosvenor Square.

There are better descriptions of this historic confrontation elsewhere and I will only relate a few episodes that remain confusedly etched in my memory. People and situations entered and disappeared from my vision, which was, like Nelson's, restricted for most of the time to one eye, as I peered through my viewfinder.

Immediately before the fracas I was most impressed and proud of the London bobby. I was in the front row of the crowd, my chest pressed against that of a young policeman, one of a link forming a human chain to protect the Embassy.

'Excuse me sir, would you please move back?' he said. I could not as the crowd behind kept pushing forward. The chain broke during this *tête-à-tête*, or to be more accurate by now, *nez-à-nez* and I was propelled forward like a novice surfer, fearfully aware of the huge wave looming behind me.

Managing to scramble clear, I sprinted along a diagonal route, avoiding the horses which had broken their formation and were charging the crowd. The police had taken a lot of provocation up to this point, ignoring the catcalls and the occasional missile. It wasn't until one of the policemen was knocked off his mount by a larger than average sod of earth and some of the demonstrators started attacking the horses that the restraint burst. It started an avalanche that devastated the good intentions of the bona fide protesters and fulfilled the hopes of those who wanted to sabotage the peace rally.

After the battle most of the combatants retired and the victims were carried away either in ambulances or police vans, but some still sat on the sidelines, unable to leave the scene. I picked my way through abandoned banners and discarded placards and leaflets calling for peace. There were piles of newspapers, broken bottles and crushed beer and soft drink cans and occasionally crumpled figures, too tired or stoned to move from the spot where they lay slumped.

I passed several friends and fellow photographers, all of us slightly dazed and wanting to be left alone. It was then I saw Marsha in one of the small groups scattered around the area and I hazily remember being introduced by her to a reticent figure who I thought was Mick Jagger. Before I had a chance to speak, some lout barged among us, grabbing Jagger by his lapels and accusing him of being at the demonstration just to get publicity. There was a scuffle and I walked away without even bothering to lift my camera. It was one of those days.

The day that Marsha came to look at the results of her session was also one of mixed emotion. She had been walking along Oxford Street on her way to the studio, eating grapes and feeling happy. Passing by a bowler-hatted, very British gentleman, she had offered him a grape, saying, 'Peace'.

'Black bitch!' he responded, ignoring her offering. 'Fuck off!'

afterthoughts...

There is a poignant photograph, reminding me of this episode every time I see it. It is of a flower child, proffering a flower in a supplication of peace, in front of the barrel of a rifle, held by a National Guard who looks at her, impassively.

I do not really understand why it moves me because I was never really a sympathiser with the peace movement. I was always slightly against flower power, always slightly sceptical.

Is there such a thing as a justifiable war? I think there is. If someone invades, do you just lie down and let them kill you? I think you must fight back.

Flower power, for me, was 'turning the other cheek' and there are people, who if you turn the other cheek, do hit it. I only attended the protest marches for picture purposes, I was on the fringe again, a voyeur, not a participant; a recorder.

I did not go to see *Hair*. I found the pop mysticism and pop philosophy left me cold. It picked up on Oriental philosophies which had perhaps taken thousands of years to develop and served them up pat.

At heart I think I am a deep-seated conservative and all the things I have done which are unconventional are really just kicking over the traces. My photography is fairly conservative because I don't like being iconoclastic just for the sake of it. I'd rather bring something more to a tradition than to break it.

I feel if one continually starts from scratch, one is often destroying something valid, and one has to build up to that valid thing again, reaching perhaps only the same level, slightly removed. I believe more in building upon than in starting afresh, but it might be a bad thing, like adding Victorian additions to a Georgian house. It becomes a hybrid.

via Western eyes...

It has not been until late in life that I have suddenly started to appreciate my Oriental side, and enjoy Oriental art. I didn't want to attach myself to it before because of the stigma of being half-Chinese. Now I recognise that my drawing has always been very flat and two-dimensional, in the Oriental manner.

In line with my father, I had always looked down upon Oriental medicine, even though my mother had often used Chinese herbs to cure us of various ills. If I had a fever, or a cold, my mother would feed me Chinese medicine. 'Don't give him that rubbish!' my father would respond. 'Give him this.'

So I sometimes had both. In the prison camp, where most medicines were unavailable, she treated a man, later to become the Governor of Singapore, for athlete's foot and cured him.

My father was very sceptical about it all, even though he had some tolerance for Chinese philosophy. There was another form of treatment that she employed, which he deplored. It consisted of breaking the blood vessels between the eyes to cure headache, or breaking the blood vessels on the back of the neck. It left a red mark for a while, which I hated because I didn't want to be disfigured, no matter how temporary it was. My father's attitudes had a big influence on me and a lot of his prejudices as well.

It meant that I could not embrace the Eastern philosophies that began to permeate attitudes in the sixties. I found it all so fake. How could a European superficially take on something in five years, that took 5,000 years to develop? I could not respond to the American hard-edged painters of the period, like Kenneth Noland and Ellsworth Kelly, because I had seen it all before in Tantric art. I could not embrace the Eastern philosphies that came via Western eyes.

A lot of the people I knew did not realise that I was half-Chinese. Sometimes people would suggest that I had American Indian blood, but one didn't volunteer what one was. There wasn't any advantage in it. I noticed the same applied to many of my acquaintances who had Indian blood, or some other mixture. People wouldn't hesitate to throw it in your face if they had something against you.

THE TATLER AND OTHER JOURNALS

The Tatler...

It was in the earliest days of my photographic career that I was introduced to a fashion photographer whose name was widely credited in magazines and newspapers. I was just starting out and was lucky enough to be employed for *The Tatler*, doing a variety of assignments. '*The Tatler*?' he questioned. 'Society shots?' he added with a sneer.

'Yes,' I stammered, in awe of the speaker, 'amongst other things.' He didn't say anything else but clearly dismissed me as a real photographer. Fashion photographers had yet to attain the superstar status that came a little later but they had already created a system or hierarchy similar to the caste system in India. Fashion was the apex, reportage a sort of halfway house, depending on the magazine one's work appeared in and press photographers were relegated to the bottom of the league, the base, the untouchable. Society photographers, even for *The Tatler*, were not much better.

Scores of the disciples of the select fashion set could be seen on their pilgrimages, along a route that stretched from Kings Road, Chelsea, to Carnaby Street, hanging outside fashion studios and fashion boutiques—stations of the cross leading to that heaven, Vogue House.

I didn't even try to justify my position and *The Tatler* served me well, both then and in the years that were to follow.

Moët... with a 't'...

Sometimes the commissions led abroad and one of the more pleasurable of these was an assignment to do a picture story on champagne.

'But I don't know anything about champagne,' I protested.

'You'll learn,' was the editor's reply. 'Have you got a valid passport?' I nodded. 'Telephone after three this afternoon... and enjoy yourself. Lucky swine!'

Later that day I dialled the number and was put through to John Verner, the public relations officer of Moët and Chandon. 'There are two return tickets to Paris waiting for you,' he informed me, 'and arrangements have been made to pick you up at Orly and transport you to Epernay to stay at the chateau for a week.'

Our son was still very young, so sadly my wife couldn't accompany me. Terry, an art school chum who had just started work as a graphic designer, was elected to come along.

Over patriotic pudding at London's exclusive Reform Club, the PR man filled me in on the details. After my second cup of coffee, I plucked up enough courage to tell him I knew very little about wine and absolutely nothing about champagne, except that it fizzed, went 'pop' when opened and last but not least, was very expensive. 'Don't worry,' said John, 'I know you can handle a camera and, as for the rest, the people over there will fill you in . . . Relax!' he added. 'Have a nice time.'

Terry and I arrived at Orly to be met by a uniformed chauffeur, standing by a luxurious limousine and holding a placard with our names on it. As soon as we were seated, the car gently slid out of the environs of the airport and soon we were speeding silently through the French countryside to Epernay.

We arrived at a formidable building, surrounded by a low wall with iron railings. Going through a large gate we halted outside a smaller building where a frail gentleman, with a hat on his head, smiled us a greeting. His eyes, peering through large horn-rimmed glasses, were twinkling.

Amidst a flurry of shaking hands and typically French embraces, we were led, without a word, to a small table in the forecourt and then seated.

The limousine reversed, with our bags still in it, and disappeared through the open gates. Seeing the alarm on my face our host smiled even more broadly and said, in an accent that made Maurice Chevalier sound like Lord Olivier: 'Welcome! Don't worry about your luggage. It is being taken to the chateau.'

My face must have been like a children's primer because he read it without the slightest hesitation. 'Ho, ho, ho,' he chortled. 'You thought this was the chateau! No, it is the museum, part of the factory and the cellars,' and he indicated the surrounding mass of buildings with a broad sweep of his arm.

He clapped his hands and immediately a young woman appeared with a bottle of champagne and three glass flutes on a silver tray. With expert fingers, he disposed of the wire cage and gently eased the cork out with a muted pop. 'A good champagne, properly chilled, should never go off like a cannon,' he informed us and touched the tip of his nose knowingly with his forefinger, giving me a conspiratorial wink.

This was my first lesson. The news of my ignorance had arrived ahead of me. I remembered John's advice and started to relax. As he filled one of the flutes, his hand seemed to hiccough slightly and the sudden surge caused the contents to overflow the rim and trickle down the side to form a little bubbly pool on the table top. 'Ah!' he exclaimed, dipping a finger into it and transporting a few drops to dab on my earlobe. 'For good luck!' he explained. 'It is a custom.'

This charming gentleman was M. René Sabber, a relative of our host proper, Count Robert de Vogue. From these two flowed an incessant stream of information in the days that followed, that enabled me to surround the pictures I took with words that made sense.

Our days began with mid-morning champagne, served on the rolling lawn in front of the chateau, then visits to vineyards and cellars, meeting the various vineyard owners and sampling their wines. On these visits, when wine and champagne were automatically produced and served, our host always added water to his glass, diluting the contents considerably.

'Some would think it sacrilegious,' I remarked on one occasion, 'to turn wine into water.'

'You see,' replied the Count, in his impeccable English, 'I have to do the rounds constantly with guests, wine buyers, visitors . . .

a thousand other reasons. If I drank all the wine full-strength on these occasions,' he paused, 'consider my kidneys!'

It was on one of these visits that he corrected my pronunciation, saying that it was 'Moë-t' not 'Mo-ay' as I had wrongly thought. 'You must sound the "t",' he informed me, 'even though many of my countrymen don't. You see Jean-Remy Moët founded the firm in 1743, and his name is always pronounced with the "t". The origin is not French as the umlaut over the "e" will testify. And,' he added, 'the "t" has continued to be sounded, in spite of the amalgamation with Chandon.'

Not wanting to make another *faux pas* I asked him how I should address him. I had been 'Lewis' since our introduction and I was uneasy in my mind. Was it *Monsieur*, or *Monsieur Le Compte*?

'Robert,' he replied, using the English pronunciation.

'Robert?' I questioned. 'You sound the "t" as in Moët?'

'*Touché*,' he said, graciously, making one more lesson for my copy which so far I had avoided blotting.

It was during the last dinner at the chateau that John's assurances to relax and enjoy myself were completely fulfilled. I was seated next to my host and we were discussing other topics, besides wine. He told me that he kept sheep, confiding that he preferred them to people as they didn't argue. The flock also served a practical purpose as the roast lamb on the menu testified.

'No doubt this one answered you back,' I commented.

'*Touché*,' he replied again.

I was fed with delectable morsels of lamb along with succinct servings of information about the intricacies of champagne and other wines as the dinner progressed. Personal revelations were also on the menu and we found that we had both been prisoners of war. But his experiences with the Nazis were much more harrowing, making my four years with the Japanese seem rather like a stay at a holiday camp. At one point, an ancient bottle of champagne, reserved for occasions like this, was brought from a cache in the cellars.

We were warned that more likely than not it would be undrinkable, but sometimes gold was dredged from the bowels of the earth. It was Russian roulette, *méthode champenoise*. More often than not, the result was disappointing.

On this occasion, the bottle's claim to quality was deemed without merit, having been tainted by its time spent in idleness. The Count was found guilty, before the fact, for raising our expectations but compensation was fully paid when a superb bottle of red wine was served with the cheese. 'Do try this,' said my host, indicating one of the cheeses, 'with this wine.'

My glass was charged with red wine that lacked the glow one usually associates with it. To my eyes it appeared positively drab. The cheese was overpowering in its pungency, not a cheese I would voluntarily have chosen. 'Try a bit and have a sip of the wine,' he encouraged me.

Never had I previously experienced the taste explosion that assailed my taste buds at that moment. What is more, it remains unequalled to the present day. I can only recount that it was sensuality personified, almost sexual. I hurriedly looked around the other guests to see that I hadn't blatantly exposed my pleasure. Here was another experience and another lesson, one of countless others generously imparted during this time.

In the euphoria of the moment, I didn't enquire of the wine that was served, or the cheese, and for several years after I experimented constantly with every sort of cheese and every sort of wine imaginable, without ever getting anywhere near the magic combination.

With hindsight, I think it fortunate that I did not find out the names of those magic ingredients. The spell may not have worked again without that other ingredient of the right people, food and surroundings. The wonderful memory may have been rendered less memorable, perhaps even destroyed, turning gold into base metal.

I think the lessons harvested at that dinner are the finest gift I received from Moët and Chandon, the final and most important lesson in being 'filled in'. There is no harm in recalling the past. The danger is in trying to relive it.

Somerset Maugham...

I was in Saint-Tropez by a ruse. Theo Goldrey, with whom I had often worked for *She* magazine, and her husband, Charles Woodham-Smith, had access to a small villa in Saint-Tropez and as they were taking their annual holiday there, the subject of an article on the *plage* was broached. This time Theo and I were collaborating for *The Tatler* and when the editor gave the article, '*Fin de Saison*', his blessing, I flew out to join them at the villa for the last days of their vacation.

It was a very enjoyable chore, lounging on the beach, lapping up the sun or a *frappe*, pointing the camera and clicking when something photogenic crossed the viewfinder.

We photographed the boutiques and cafés, the flower market and the up-market villas of the social butterflies. On one occasion, Kenneth More and Jack Hawkins got in the way of the camera and cavorted in front of the lens, pulling out their empty trouser pockets to mime their financial state.

The last location on our list was the grand villa La Fiorentina, home of the Countess of Kenmere. After I had finished photographing her, Lady Kenmere introduced us to her son, the author Roderick Cameron, who had retreated to the quiet of the villa at Cap Ferrat, to work on his book about Captain Cook.

We joined him for tea, which he poured from a silver teapot, into porcelain cups. In between sips, he casually mentioned that he was to play cards with his neighbour, Somerset Maugham, adding as an afterthought, 'Now that you are here, would you like to photograph him?' Eager nods greeted this suggestion.

He picked up the telephone on the side table next to him and dialled a number. After a few short rings, the call was answered.

'Alan? . . . Roderick. Got some people from *The Tatler*, would like to photogra . . . Yes, I should think so.' He covered the mouthpiece. 'Can you get up to the villa later this afternoon? . . . Yes? OK . . . Yes Alan, they'll be along after tea.' He replaced the phone. 'Alan would like to meet you later on to arrange a meeting.'

It would seem that Alan, Maugham's 'man Friday' was a buffer between the writer and the outside world, filtering the acceptable morsels from the dross that piled itself at the gates of the Villa Mauresque, hoping to get an audience, or just a glimpse of the grand old man of literature.

A short time later, Alan Searle let us through the heavy doors, set into the high wall that ran around the property. Searle, who had lived with Maugham for many years, was his adopted son, even though Maugham did have children of his own. The writer wasn't due back till much later and it was arranged that we would return the next morning at eleven, to meet him. We had passed the litmus test and were deemed acceptable by Alan, who was no doubt echoing the selectivity of his mentor.

During this preliminary inquisition, we were shown around the grounds and then led to the large swimming pool, set in the garden. 'Would you like to swim?' Alan asked. We told him we had not come prepared and that we did not have any bathing costumes with us. 'Oh, don't worry about that!' he shrugged. 'We've got plenty of towels.' But we turned the offer down, in the politest possible way, not being sure what it implied.

The next morning, on the dot of eleven, we were once again at the Villa Mauresque and were led again to the garden with the swimming pool. This time here was the man himself, seated in a cane chair, wearing an open-neck striped shirt, a glossy dachshund on his lap. He rose, spilling the dog from his lap. We shook hands and introduced ourselves under the protective ministrations of Alan, hovering and fluttering by turns, as circumstances demanded.

Theo, Charles and myself sat down, forming an inverted triangle facing Maugham, in a classic, acolyte to master formation. He looked fragile, even brittle as his was not a soft face. It was a face that could be cruel, yet with an element of defensiveness, set on top of a neck that was drawn taut with tendons. It reminded me of a turtle's and yes, the head itself was that of a turtle, but the vision of a turtle on its back, unable to flip itself upright, kept crossing my mind.

It was as if the armour of words and barbs that the younger Maugham had once shielded behind was now only a worn facsimile of the original. The feeling that a good, sharp blast of invective, or an intrusive question could penetrate and lay him low, was no doubt falsely suggested by his fragile state. There was still plenty of fire left.

Conversation was difficult. He frequently stuttered and hesitated in his replies, owing to a recent stroke from which he had not fully recovered. I photographed while Theo gently tested the water with lukewarm questions, carefully, in case she was out of her depth and had to tread water in an icy reply. She avoided the more delicate ones which would have been out of place for this feature but which I am sure she would have loved to ask to satisfy her journalistic curiosity.

In the course of describing his garden, he pointed to a low hill that overlooked part of his estate, and expressed his displeasure that someone had purchased it, with the intention of building a villa.

'At least you'll have some neighbours,' I ventured.

'Neighbours!' he snorted. 'I don't want neighbours! They'll be overlooking my pool.'

He hesitated to catch his breath and vent his anger. 'But I've put paid to that! I've planted trees to block their view,' he declared triumphantly, indicating the area with his outflung arm. There, in a neat row, stood an array of minute saplings. They would take at least thirty years to provide the screen that he intended. He was over his three score and ten at this time and I was both amused and touched by his optimism.

He calmed down and the conversation took a gentler tack but the outburst and the activity had tired him and rising from his seat, he said he would have to take a little rest. I had finished photographing and was putting my camera into the case while he stood, addressing no one in particular. 'So many people have photographed me,' he mused, 'but I never receive a photograph from any of the sessions.'

'I'll make sure you get one from me,' I promised. 'I'll personally post you some as soon as they are processed.'

'That's very kind,' he replied. 'I'll look forward to seeing them.' And he bade us farewell and slowly made his way to the villa, attended by his dachshund. As he was just about to disappear through the French windows, I stopped my camera's casebound journey long enough to take one last shot of the receding, striped shirt.

Alan Searle saw us to the car. As I was about to get in he told me not to send the photographs to Cap Ferrat. 'I'll be in London next month,' he added. 'Give me your phone number and I'll contact you.'

Within the month I got the promised call from Alan, who asked me to meet him at his hotel and to bring the photographs with me. This I did. I had enlarged three of the ones that I thought epitomised Maugham's persona.

'They're very good,' said Alan when he saw them. 'It's him but I don't think I can show them to him. They're too honest.'

I didn't know whether to be offended or flattered. In any case, Alan kept them.

I could now understand the reason behind Maugham's complaint. He probably never saw the bulk of the photographs taken of him, even though they were duly sent. Alan, the filterer, saw to that.

When the Saint-Tropez article was published, the Maugham photograph was not included. I was a little upset and phoned up the editorial staff to find out the reason. 'There was nothing wrong with the photo,' I was told. 'How about lunch?'

Over lunch they told me that one of the upper echelons in management was very anti-Maugham . . . something to do with his private lifestyle. I didn't delve any further. People have a funny way of getting even and vetoing a photograph was one.

Renishaw unvisited...

It was one of those English invitations... 'Well then,' said Sir Osbert, 'you must pay us a visit soon,' which is not an invitation at all, but in its cloaked English ambiguity, really a statement left hovering in the limbo of polite parting manners. So my visit to Renishaw, country house of the Sitwell family, did not come about until two decades after Sir Osbert's death.

The Tatler had sent Ronald Blythe and myself to interview and photograph Sitwell. Blythe was no stranger to Sir Osbert and had recollections of dining with him at No 2 Carlyle Square, a William IV house just off the King's Road, Chelsea. This was the residence where in 1922, a select audience saw and heard the first performance of *Facade*, the nonsense verses of Edith Sitwell, set to William Walton's currently faddish, jazz-oriented music. The words had been shouted through a megaphone from behind a screen with holes in it, the screen being painted by the sculptor, Frank Dobson. But that house was now only a memory. Sir Osbert had recently moved into a large flat on the second floor of a gloomy late Edwardian mansion, York House. With him came the gilt furniture and marble tables, the paintings and other *objets d'art*, and his long standing companion, David Horner.

Although large and airy, the flat had already acquired a cocooned quality, reminiscent of a fly in amber. Although there were no cobwebs, there was a musty, unlived-in order. Not unoccupied, but unlived. One existed in this atmosphere, one did not participate. It was a sanitised Miss Haversham house and I sensed a miasma of emotions, both angry and sad. The sun through the large windows belied the dark overtones pervading every room. Everything seemed frozen in time. One was not aware of the clocks ticking and here I was in 1963 looking at the originals of things I had seen in photographs taken in the 1920s. Paintings by Chirico and Braque, John Piper drawings, bronze and wood sculptures, Greek terracottas and a magnificent St John the Baptist by Raphael.

In the years that followed, every time I was reminded of the Sitwells, these images kept appearing in my mind, in half-tones made up of blacks and greys of varying intensity and sharpness —an amorphous kaleidoscope of furniture, artefacts, sculptures, paintings and drawings that I had seen in other people's photographs and was now seeing *in situ* at York House.

Sir Osbert was wheeled into the large room by David Horner. He was dressed in varying shades of grey, slumped in his wheelchair, grasping his cane and apparently oblivious to all around him. The mid-grey double-breasted suit had a faint Prince of Wales check running through it. His shirt was of the palest pearl grey and the grey silk tie had a pattern of broken bars like a Wadsworth woodcut of the camouflaged World War I ships. It was a design that his *friend*, Wyndham Lewis, would have approved.

Their presence in London was due to a fall David Horner had had during an uneasy stay at Montegufoni, the Sitwells' Italian *castello*. Also present were Sir Osbert, who was deeply attached to him, and Dame Edith, who disliked him intensely. Horner had fallen, or as he claimed, been pushed, by someone living or dead, down a flight of stone steps, and had broken his arm and several ribs. Sir Obsert was confined to his wheelchair and was suffering from Parkinson's disease, and as it was imperative for both of them to be close to treatment in London, York House was the obvious solution.

Horner, with one arm in a sling, managed to manoeuvre Sir Osbert into the centre of the room where I was engaged loading my camera. He was also acquainted with Ronald Blythe whom he had not seen for some time, so the two left the room to chat, leaving me alone with Sir Osbert and yet to be introduced.

I was a little embarrassed as he was trembling from his ailment and a slight trickle of saliva escaped from the corner of his mouth. He seemed, as I thought, unaware of my presence, so I continued to busy myself, loading and fussing with the camera. There was a gentle cough. 'You can speak to me if you wish young man,' came a hesitant voice. I was taken unawares and said the first thing that came into my mind.

'I like your Tchelitchew.' When I had arrived, I'd noticed a striking portrait of Dame Edith Sitwell by Pavel Tchelitchew, and it was still fresh in my mind.

'Oh good,' he said, and with a small scooping motion of his hand, he beckoned me to approach him. 'Come here and get me out of this.'

I left my photographic paraphernalia and walked across the room to his wheelchair. 'Here,' he said, lifting his arms, 'get me up.'

I placed my arms around his ample frame and heaved. After a struggle I got him to his feet, then he put his arm around me to support himself and with the aid of his cane proceeded to give me a guided tour through the various rooms, showing me all his paintings and sculptures.

He was pleased when I expressed my amazement at his collection of Callots. 'Oh, you recognise the Callots?' And it was heart-warming to see the joy he obviously got from an appreciative audience. He told me the merits of the New Ireland sculpture that hung next to what I recall was an Arthur Boyd painting, and spoke about the relationship between the primitive and modern art to me. His words, the Nadelmann bronze and the marble-topped tables, the milk glass and the ormolu, the abundant collection festooning the walls and placed around all the rooms, blended to form a confused but lasting impression which would inexplicably surface from time to time.

He showed me a wardrobe, the surface of which represented the contents inside. Jackets and trousers on hangers, rendered in a fairly impasto manner.

'It obviously isn't a Sickert,' I ventured, 'but whoever painted it was certainly influenced by the master.'

'Yes, the artist was,' he said. 'It was inevitable, she was one of his more talented students.'

Encouraged by my success I pointed out another painting and remarked that I'd never seen that particular Chirico before. He chided me for mistaking a Loudon Sainthill for a Chirico, but hastened to add that this work was heavily influenced by Chirico, both in style and subject matter, therefore my error was totally justified. What a gentlemanly way to eliminate a *faux pas*. The perfect dental surgeon, able to extract a foot from a mouth painlessly.

The conducted tour exhausted him and he had to be reseated in his wheelchair, but he seemed nevertheless pleased with the outcome of the ordeal. It had given him pleasure to show an appreciative stranger his prized objects. While we were photographing he confided to me, 'I dislike London. I miss being at Renishaw. Have you been to Renishaw?' I shook my head. 'Well then, you must pay us a visit soon.'

Soon was twenty years, but that's another story.

metamorphosis... Salvador Dali...

'You'll never make a press photographer,' said Ted Spooner, the picture editor of the *Daily Express*.

'But I don't want to be one,' I replied.

It was in the early days of my photographic career and I had managed to have several photographs of newsworthy, pretty girls published in the William Hickey column. Reportage photography was, at that time, my burning ambition and it was Cartier Bresson I wanted to emulate, capturing 'the moment' simply but unobtrusively. I had no desire to be a brash newspaper photographer, barging in and clicking away to get the picture, regardless of the sensibilities of the subject.

'Even if you did, you couldn't,' Spooner continued.

'Why not?' I countered, getting angry now.

'Because you haven't got the elbows!' he replied, rejecting my latest submission, a photograph of Cecil Beaton that later found its way into the National Portrait Gallery's collection.

I didn't have the opportunity or the heart to ask him what he meant by elbows but it wasn't too long before I found out with a vengeance. A freelance journalist friend told me that Salvador Dali was due to arrive at Victoria Station and wanted to know if I could grab a couple of shots for him for a proposed article. I hated these 'commissions' from friends. You were made to feel guilty if you turned them down, but if you agreed, you knew that you were up for the price of the materials and your time. If, and only if they were successful in placing the article would any form of reimbursement be considered. Some would get a picture credit for you and consider that payment enough for your efforts and financial outlay. However, this time I needed no prompting. If I could get a couple of good pictures of Dali for my portfolio, that would be reward enough.

By mistake, I got to Victoria Station an hour before the train was due to arrive, but even then I noticed that there were quite a few early hopefuls, clutching cameras that ranged from box Brownies to Hasselblads. They were mostly amateurs. The boys from the Press had not yet started to muster. I knew from experience that if I decided to come back later it would be impossible to break through their serried ranks. Along with the police, an inevitable presence on these occasions, these ranks would quickly harden into an impenetrable wall.

As the enthusiastic amateurs waited patiently by the arrival board, chatting to each other and comparing their cameras. I hid mine under my duffle coat and found out on which platform the boat train from Paris was to arrive. Then I bought a platform ticket and a newspaper and settled down to wait for it.

About five minutes before the appointed time, an implosion of camera-carrying pressmen converged on the target area. The train chuffed into the bay and squealed to a halt.

A door was opened and there was Dali, leaning out, holding aloft his silver-mounted cane. Flash guns discharged fusillade after fusillade of man-made lightning, as if the man with the moustache were a lightning conductor.

The platform was crammed. As I had been in position before the invasion, I had the advantage of being in the front row, clicking away, adding my hesitant shuttering to the cacophony of the other weapons, fired at will.

I managed to shoot about ten frames of Dali, accompanied by a handsome woman, enigmatically wearing dark glasses on this grey day, miles from summer. Then a painful jab in the ribs spun me round, only to be checked by a sharp blow to the jaw. As my mind cleared, my watery eyes managed to focus on the weapons that had been used to dispossess me of my front-line position. Not swung cameras or flash guns as I first suspected, but elbows! Yes, Mr Spooner was unerringly accurate in his assessment of me and I was now relegated to the back row. I didn't have the elbows.

Counterattack was out of the question, but I was not going to give up that easily. I figured that Dali and his entourage must pass through the only car exit, so I positioned myself at a standpoint where I would have a clear field of fire. How wrong I was! The Rolls Royce emerged but the attacking hordes kept pace with its slow advance to freedom. They jogged alongside the car, shooting through the windscreen and every available window. A shot from my position was impossible. I groaned softly to myself, lowered my camera and was turning to leave when I was attracted by the sound of tapping on the Rolls' window.

The car had stopped and the window was being lowered. The other photographers immediately recognised that my vantage point was now desirable and before you could say 'Cheese!' I was once again engaged in the battle of the elbows. This time I conceded defeat. For me, the war had ended. I didn't resume my low-key assault on Mr Dali and was surprised when the shaded lady beckoned me to approach. I was surrounded by a shoal of 'snappers' and was not entirely certain she meant me, so I pointed to myself and raised an enquiring eyebrow. She nodded vigorously and impatiently beckoned me again. I hurried to the open window. 'Would you like to photograph Mr Dali? Come to my apartment at The Albany. Just tell the doorman that you are visiting me, he will tell you where to go.'

She flashed me a smile and told the driver to continue. Salvador Dali and the others in the packed car looked at me curiously but said not a word. I was dumbfounded, then suddenly struck with an awful thought: *Who was 'me'*?

I couldn't approach The Albany's custodian and say that a lady, whose name I did not know, had asked me to visit her. In my panic I started to run after the car which was rapidly pulling away. I hailed an empty taxi and almost threw myself under the wheels to make sure it stopped. It did, and with an uninhibited oath from the cabbie I flung myself onto the back seat and slammed the door. For the first and only time in my life, I uttered the immortal words: 'Follow that car!' But there was no frantic, exciting car chase across the metropolis. London traffic saw to that. We caught up with our quarry and followed it, our bumper bar glued to the exhaust pipe of the Rolls Royce.

The cars arrived at The Albany simultaneously. I paid my cab and caught up with them on the stairs. We were met outside the entrance of the shaded lady's apartment by a photographer and a female journalist. 'What are you doing here with those cameras?' she cried. 'We're from the *Express* and we have an exclusive. Who are you?'

The shaded lady gave the irate journalist a long cool stare and answered for me. 'Do you mind! This is my guest. Please get on with what you have to do as quickly as possible.'

A short, tense interview ensued, followed by an even shorter and more embarrassing photo session between Dali and the press photographer. The photographer wanted the 'mad' Dali but the artist declined to act zany, saying that he couldn't in a room like this. '... with my rhinoceros perhaps, but not here,' he added, confusing the photographer even further.

Twenty-five years before he would have acted zany any place, any time, with or without his rhinoceros. Nevertheless, he compromised with one or two Daliesque poses. The duo from the *Express* wanted him to live out his myth, but this he was no longer willing to do. They finished their business and were ushered out of the apartment. As the door closed behind them, the suppressed anxiety gave way to an audible sigh of relief. My hostess turned to me and asked for my name.

'Lewis Morley,' I replied.

'I am Fleur Cowles,' she continued, 'and this is Mr Salvador Dali.' I shook hands with both in turn. 'He's all yours,' she said and left it to me to do as I wished.

In place of the mad, fakir-eyed, panther-lean, sensation hungry Dali of the 1930s, I saw an older, heavier but none-theless, impressive man, with a dignity that belied his reputation for 5th Avenue window smashing and dressing up in diving suits.

He seemed weary but this was not surprising after a trip from Paris. Also he had been constantly sniped at by the photographers who had accompanied him on the train from Dover. In the comparative privacy of the apartment, the professional 'mad gleam' was momentarily banished and a withdrawn look took over. There were occasional flickers of anguish which transformed his face so that it resembled that of a crucified Christ in a medieval painting. It was as if a war of conflicting motives was raging within him. I felt that here was a painter, trying to paint more seriously than he had ever done before. If he was still controlled by gimmicks, it was because Dali had entered his own labyrinth and although he knew the way out, he could not escape because the exit was guarded by the publicity Minotaur. It was the clown, wanting to play Hamlet but forbidden to because he was Hamlet.

I noticed a carved Madonna and Child and asked him if he would sit beside it. It seemed more appropriate to the Dali of today. He accepted with a majestic graciousness that made the resemblance between him and Velasquez's

Philip IV more obvious than just the moustache. I placed his head close to the sculpture and he gave me one of those famous Dali stares. I shot off a few frames and looked up. Thinking I had finished, he immediately relaxed and a totally different expression replaced the artificially induced mask that he so often hid behind. Without looking down to refocus I instinctively shifted the camera to match his movement as he straightened up from the slightly crouched position he had been in. The result is an exposure with a very slight blurring of the image. I prefer it to all the other Madonna shots. It was, I felt, the moment of truth.

The friend who had asked me to photograph Dali found that he couldn't arrange an interview for his article, and so conveniently forgot that he had commissioned me. Nothing more was said regarding the assignment, or the expenses involved. A glossy magazine contacted me and used two of the photographs. Their fee more than covered the time and money spent and as a bonus I now had the photographs of Dali for my archives.

postscript...

In the years since this episode I have been asked, at various times, why, of all the photographers that were milling around, Fleur Cowles had picked on me. The question had also puzzled me and it was not until the late 1980s, when I was preparing for my exhibition at The National Portrait Gallery that I came closer to a solution.

In the mountain of negatives which I was sorting through to find suitable images for the exhibition were the contact prints of the Dali session, wrapped around the negatives of the session themselves. For the first time, I actually studied them closely. Previously, the only images that had interested me were the close-ups, the arrival pictures at the station were not considered. Every photographer at the meeting had taken virtually the same shots and therefore I had ignored them.

Now, I took a magnifying glass to them to see if there was a shot worthy of enlargement. It came as a shock to discover that in many of the frames both Dali and especially Fleur Cowles, were looking straight at me. Not towards the camera but straight at the photographer. I am still uncertain why the very personal exchanges that took place in those few seconds, generated the impulse for Fleur Cowles to target me from all the others. Perhaps I was simply the least offensive, of the offensive.

London preserved...

The satirical magazine, *Private Eye*, shared part of the top floor of my new premises, storing a lot of their back issues and consumer goods in the spare room next to my reception. It was a reciprocal gesture as I made use of their premises as a location for a Swiss fashion catalogue, photographing models *in situ*, and incorporating Tony Rushton and Richard Ingrams as living props.

It was through them that I first met John Betjeman, a member of that quintessentially English club, the eccentric. We collaborated on a series of mini-articles for *Private Eye*, the theme being the unsuitability of much of the modern architecture that was destroying the landscape. The articles were to single out some of the more awful blots . . . a *Private Eye*'s List of Public Eyesores, erupting unchecked like fresh ulcers on the already blemished London landscape.

Over tea we discussed some of the more outrageous Goliaths which confronted this David, armed with only a quill to do battle, while my camera was to record the campaign. Betjeman was an affable creature, unless he was riled over some matter about which he felt strongly, like contemporary architecture. Then, he would attach himself to the subject like a terrier, sinking his teeth in and holding on, like that other quintessentially English animal, the bulldog. He was like a posh Cockney 'sparrer', not born within sound of Bow Bells, not even living within reach of the famous chimes, but in some way, such a part of London that he was a Cockney by default.

Not the most elegant of dressers on the occasions I worked with him, with his hat set jauntily on his head and his raincoat flying open, his eyes would be darting left and right, taking in all that was to be seen. Chirpy would be the most apt description for him, making him more the sparrow than the peacock, though on occasions he could show great dignity without pomposity. Then he had the demeanour of a plump hawk, quiet and still, apparently oblivious to his surroundings. Yet one knew that his mind was going nineteen to the dozen and nothing was escaping his twinkling eye as he assessed his beloved London. His joy and his sadness at this metropolis which was so much a part of him made his concern that the heritage should continue, all the stronger. He bemoaned the buildings that should have been kept, but hadn't, and the buildings that were going up, that shouldn't. His continual struggle was to prevent the philistines from pilfering, squandering and destroying the gems from Britain's architectural crown.

We spent many pleasant days going to unpleasant sites. I preserved them on film, he demolished them with words. During this process I was invited back to his house for tea, where his secretary joined us. When my eyes had become accustomed to the rather gloomy room, I was surprised to see another occupant whom I had not previously noticed, in the chair next to his. It was a teddy bear, rather beaten-up, but very dignified. I was about to make an awful pun about picnics but something stopped me. I had already made one *faux pas* by wrongly attributing to him a poem with the line 'And is there honey still for tea,' which I had made worse by quoting.

Tea was served but I declined the offer of scotch from the crystal decanter that Betjeman held towards me. He filled himself a small glass, solemnly raising it to me, then to Teddy, took a drink and put the glass to Teddy's lips to give him a sip. This was repeated until the glass was empty. His secretary, busying herself pouring tea, buttering the scones and making social noises, showed no sign that anything was amiss. The whole ritual, for that is what it was, was then repeated when Betjeman had a refill. I finished my tea and we left the table for the sitting room to continue our discussion of the day's work. Teddy remained in his seat.

I do not know to this day whether the teddy episode was a genuine occurrence which took place each teatime, or whether I was the victim of a very wry practical joke. I have not to date met another person who had tea with John Betjeman and his teddy bear to enlighten me.[1]

Later, when Betjeman found out that I was emigrating to Australia, he advised me, 'If you are to live in Sydney, make sure to live in Paddington.' When I arrived in Sydney in 1971, I visited Paddington and saw the terrace houses with their balconies of cast-iron lace, and ups and downs of the wide roads and the twists and turns of the narrow lanes. It was so much like his poetry but much as I admired that, I must admit that his choice of a place to live was not my cup of tea, or small glass of whiskey if it came to that.

Just before leaving the UK I received a letter from him. His appreciation of our brief collaboration on the cement monsters of London was literally put into concrete form in the shape of a small poem, dedicated to 'My Ally in Architecture'. It was only a stanza but it showed his concern for others and a genuine sense of pleasure for the shared experience of our working together.

Like some of the architectural treasures he tried to preserve, Betjeman is no longer with us, but because of his untiring efforts, certain buildings have continued to exist. I feel sure that the appreciation of all who have benefited and continue to benefit from his heroic struggles will increase and survive, beyond the edifices that he helped to preserve.

1. Humphrey Carpenter, in *The Brideshead Generation* notes that Betjeman's teddy 'Archie' was the inspiration for Sebastian Flyte's teddy, 'Aloysius' in Evelyn Waugh's *Brideshead Revisited.*

For Lewis Morley, my ally in architecture
from John Betjeman

I Made hay
while the sun
shone;
My writing sold;
Now if the harvest is over
And the world cold
Let me not cease to be
grateful
As I lose hold.

A WEMBLEY LAD

To every ducal palace
When days were old and slow
Me and my sister Alice
By charabanc would go.

My new position such is
In halls of social fame
That many a duke and duchess
I know by Christian name.

Belvoir, Blenheim, Chatsworth,
Luncheon, dinner, tea,
And stay the night – oh! that's worth
All the world to me.

And as for sister Alice
She is not suited here
She would not grace a palace
She'd call the duchess "dear".

I'm off to a smart assembly
With head and heart held high
But palaceless Alice in Wembley
Knows how alone go I.

THE CREM

Between the swimming bath and Cricket ground
How straight the crematorium driveway lies!
And every half an hour a puff of smoke
Shows what we loved dissolving in the skies,
Dear hands and feet and laughter-lighted eyes!

And no one seems to know quite what to say;
Friends are so altered by the passing years:
"Well anyhow it's not so cold today"
And thus we try to dissipate our fears.
—"I am the Resurrection and the Life"—
Strong, deep and certain, grief inserts the knife.

off my chest and out of my mind...

In his essay 'On Painting', Lawrence, D.H. that is, not the burnoused, violated, white Arab, accused his whipping boy, the bourgeoisie, of fig-leafing their mouths and scratching their dirty little secrets. I, too, scratched the wounds of my 'dirty little secret' every time I recalled the narrow escape I had from crossing words with John Betjeman. But unlike the Turked T.E. I didn't relish the sweet agony of guilt and physical discomfort arising from a ravished conscience.

It all started with the completion of my collaboration with John Betjeman. One of our targets had been the desecration of St Paul's vista with the newly erected, ill-designed buildings in Paternoster Square. The day I had photographed this affront, in front of Wren's masterpiece, it was pouring with rain and the uneven flagstones had taken on the appearance of a lagoon. The misty, shrouded St Paul's took on the appearance of the Chiesa Santa Maria Della Salute, floating on fog at the mouth of the Grand Canal, a vision seen on one of my visits to Venice. The fantasy had inspired me to pen a few words, which I intended enclosing with an enlargement of the photograph, and which Betjeman needed for his copy.

At the last moment I thought better of including the so-called poem with the photographs, apprehensive at exposing my embryonic efforts to an acknowledged master of the genre.

In the post, a couple of days later, arrived a printed broadsheet of Betjeman's poems and hand-written, on the space at the top, was a little poem dedicated to me for the part I had played as his ally in the crusade against the architectural philistines.

I always feel uncomfortable when I recall that occasion, at the misunderstanding that could have arisen from my poetic attempts arriving in his postbox after he had dispatched his gift to me. It could have been misconstrued as a 'So there!' reply to his thoughtful offering.

As Sir John Betjeman, the Poet Laureate, is no longer with us and it is not possible for him to be offended, scornful or at least amused by my impertinence at invading his territory, I hope to exorcise my guilty ghost by getting it out of the closet and airing it, for better or for worse.

ATONES OF VENICE

Half close your eyes
and through
the falling rain
pretend
you're Canaletto
And see St Paul's
an upside-down
Santa Maria Della Salute
reflected in
the Grand Canal
created by uneven flags
that pave
the undrained square
A shallow moat
quite deep enough
to wet your shoes
Yet not suffice
to float
A paper boat
let alone
a gondola
Paternoster Square
Or Piazza
Paternoster
Whoa..............
Hold your St Mark's Horses
and check the urge
to be drunk
on imagination's wine
remembering that—
A rose

by any other name
is still
A Gertrude Stein.

Half close your eyes
and through the rain
that falls
even Ruskin
would admit . . .
T'is a shocking mass
that overwhelms
St Paul's.

Postscript: the fact that I have lost both the photograph and negative of this image which I hold dear, and that I am now left only with this rediscovered gauche effort at versifying is, I suppose, poetic justice!

the *London American*...

The *London American* was a weekly newspaper especially printed for Americans living in, or visiting London and Larry Thaw was the expatriate American who was deeply involved with its production. Somehow, I ended up doing the photographs that illustrated the articles and interviews he wrote.

It was a labour of love, in that I loved photographing the people Larry put before my lens, and also in the sporting sense, in that the remunerative returns were 'love'. Well, not quite nil, as the *quid pro quo* proved satisfactory.

Because of the specialised nature of the *London American* and Larry's contacts, he managed to get interviews with high-profile identities, denied to many other more popular magazines and papers. André Previn, Aaron Copland, Alan J. Lerner, Al Capp, the Andrews Sisters, Clive Barnes and Eartha Kitt were just some of the people who came before my lens for this purpose.

Not all my photographs for this publication were of a quality I would have liked. There were times when the sessions resulted in a shambles. The Leontyne Price shots were one such example.

She was the first black Aida, that is, discounting the original on whom Verdi based his opera, and I had to go backstage to photograph her at the Royal Opera House, Covent Garden.

I hadn't attended the opera and when I got to her dressing-room after curtain-down, it was a fairly chaotic affair, with lots of people milling around. In due course I was pushed forward and introduced to her.

'Let me introduce you to a dear friend of mine,' she said, indicating a lanky youth, dressed in a beautifully cut suit. He was sitting in one of the dressing-room chairs, regarding the scene over clasped hands, the index fingers and thumbs forming a church steeple. His tight curly hair reminded me of an Airedale, a resemblance made even more apparent by the way he eagerly leapt up, holding out his long slim fingers to shake hands. I grasped his hand in a firm grip and gave it a hearty shake, as Leontyne Price continued: '. . . dear friend of mine who has just won the Tchaikovski Prize, Van Cliburn.'

As the last syllable left her lips, I felt his fingers pulling away from my grip. He extricated them with a grimace and was now fanning them in rapid flutters, as if to cool them or to flick the joints back into position.

He smiled at me, acknowledging Miss Price's introduction, at the same time, glancing at his fingers, still in motion, only now as though playing the scales.

I realised I had crushed his tools of trade in the same way some oaf might take my camera to peep through the view-finder and then drop it onto a concrete floor.

I stuttered a few words of congratulation on his achievement in Moscow and set about taking some photographs to cover the assignment and my confusion. I felt as crushed as his hand, waiting to 'shoot off' in both senses, as I took some singles and a few double portraits of the pair.

As I prepared to leave, Van Cliburn reached out his arm to me in an offer to shake hands. At the last moment he closed his fist, leaving only the little finger extended. I took it between my forefinger and thumb and gently waggled it. We both grinned, understanding each other perfectly.

kitten with clause... Eartha Kitt...

The vision of a purring feline atop satin sheets, pleading with Santa Baby in a low crooning voice, and concealing claws that could be exposed at the drop of an eyelid, was uppermost in my mind when I met Eartha Kitt.

The voice that answered questions during the press conference was quiet, controlled and relaxed, seasoned with a liberal sprinkling of sharp humour. The overt sexuality that oozed from the voice and the skin-tight costumes worn during her cabaret and screen appearances was less evident but nonetheless cunningly implied, rationed out between questions and quips, punctuated by flashes from the camera and the singer's smiles.

After the meeting had broken up, I approached her and introduced myself as the photographer for a previously arranged session. She suggested that we leave the main room where the conference had taken place and where journos were still milling around, finishing off a few sandwiches that were curling at the edges.

We retired to her private room where we could work uninterrupted. On our way, we were accosted by a sparrow-like Indian reporter, asking in a voice that would have made Peter Sellers shudder: 'Miss Kitt, does it upset you to be married to a white man?' Kitt had sometime in the previous few days, married a white American, causing quite a few raised eyebrows, and in the case of this Indian hack, his hackles. She stopped in her tracks and confronted him, looking him squarely in the eyes, a feat only made possible by their matching sizes.

'No,' she said curtly, dismissing him, 'it doesn't bother me but it obviously bothers you.' Then she turned on her heel and walked away leaving him rooted to the spot, momentarily speechless. He hurriedly caught up with me, grabbing my arm.

'Take a photograph for me, I will pay you,' he said. I tore my arm free. 'Piss off!'

Then I joined Eartha, who was holding the door open for me, a door which I slammed unceremoniously in his face as he attempted to follow.

Her session, like that of many true professionals, went without a hitch, devoid of the temperament that plagued a lot of the less talented. Thanking her, I took leave, only to be waylaid by the reporter who had been waiting for me outside the closed door.

'Sell me a photograph for my paper,' he arrogantly demanded.

'Not for a million pounds,' I replied.

forsaking the West... Clint Eastwood...

It was Larry Thaw who commissioned me to photograph Clint Eastwood, suggesting that if I could also get a shot of Mary Ure at the same time, it would be a bonus. Both were appearing in the same film, *Where Eagles Dare*, which was being shot at Elstree.

No problems were anticipated with Mary. I had worked with her previously at the Royal Court, but Clint Eastwood was another matter as I had been warned by Public Relations that the film was behind schedule and Eastwood was preoccupied with domestic affairs.

I arrived on location during a break in shooting and as I made my way towards the studio to track down my quarry, I had to step over a contingent of tea drinkers, all sporting German uniforms. There were greetings of 'Hi Lewis!' from the various slumped, seated and standing troops, all friends and work acquaintances from the theatre.

'What are you doing here?' questioned one.

'I'm supposed to be photographing Clint Eastwood and Mary Ure,' I replied.

'You'll be lucky!' they all chorused.

'How about Burton?' another enquired.

'No, not him,' I said.

'Just as well,' was the rejoinder, followed by gales of laughter and then I caught sight of Richard Burton, looking very unapproachable. I was glad he was not on my agenda.

'Oh, there you are,' said the public relations man, hurrying towards me. 'I've had a word with Clint and he says it's OK. He's on the phone to his wife at present and will be with you in a couple of minutes. Wait for him by the truck in the back lot.'

Sure enough, no sooner had I arrived there, than a tall figure in a Nazi uniform strode towards me, with outstretched hand, his broad smile nullifying the sinister associations of his costume. I took his hand and introduced myself.

Although I am by no means a shortie at 6 ft 1 inch, I felt dwarfed by his 6 ft 4 inch-presence. It may have been his larger than life personality that seemed to add extra inches to his more than adequate frame. Tall, lean, rugged . . . all the clichés to describe the mythical American cowboy who rocketed to fame via the Spaghetti Western. Whatever myth surrounded him was overshadowed by the reality of his looks and his meteoric rise to fame. Added to this was a genuinely warm manner that put men immediately at ease, while his charismatic screen presence, with its overtones of sexuality and its undertones of sadism, made women weak at the knees. At Elstree it wasn't only the baddies he was fighting, but time. Between a long distance call and a 'take', he took time off to comply with my needs.

It was a terse but not a tense session. He was relaxed in front of the camera, a 'natural'. Contrary to popular belief, not all actors who appear so laid back on screen, are as reposed when confronted by a still camera.

In between shots he admitted that he was missing home, his wife and his, as yet unseen, newborn son. He spoke about his next film. It was a musical, quite different from anything he had previously done and he was looking forward to it. The fact that they were two weeks behind schedule in the filming and that he was due to fly back to the States the next day, seemed not to faze him at all. Throughout the session he was the most compliant of sitters. The sitting, or to be more precise, the standing, though short, went without a hitch and I remember it as one of the easiest photo-calls in the showbiz side of my career.

The rapidity of the process left him slightly bewildered. 'Gee,' he said, in a voice of undisguised admiration. 'You finished? That's the shortest and most painless call I've ever had. Glad to do business with you . . . any time.'

Once again that large smile, shaking his hand with incredulity, as he took my hand. 'Thank you,' he said, with the kind of sincerity that made you feel good, and with a farewell wave he hurried back to the set for another take.

from a sentence to a word...

Photographing an actor *in situ* is easier because they can assume the role they're taking, even while still wanting to look their best. But an actor in civilian clothes, so to speak, projects what he thinks he should look like. We're used to thinking of Clint Eastwood, for instance, as a tough-guy, but he might think of himself as a rather aesthetic fellow. So, there's sometimes a slight battle. The actor is doing one thing while you, the photographer, want him to do another.

If you're doing it for a job you have to take what the publicist, or whoever, wants, but if you're doing it for yourself, then you photograph the person the way you think he really is. It's harder to lie to a still camera than to a movie camera. With moving film you have a sequence of images but if the movie camera is a sentence, then the still camera is a word.

Mary, Mary, quite contrary...

In life, never take everything for granted. In showbiz never take ANYTHING for granted. I assumed there would be no worries with Mary Ure and anticipated problems with Eastwood. Just the opposite transpired. If Eastwood's encounter was a dream, Mary's was a nightmare.

On our previous meetings, she had been beautiful, both in face and manner and we had got on famously. I genuinely admired her acting and she reciprocated with a regard for my photography.

On a subsequent occasion, during a rather sticky time in her career she invited me round to take some photos of her new baby. At that time she was involved with Robert Shaw and had just given birth to his child. They had yet to marry and the tabloids were having a field day. I arrived at her house to find it besieged by reporters and press photographers, apparently a daily occurrence. I literally had to fight my way through Fleet Street's vilest to get to her.

I knocked at the door and after a short delay it opened slightly and an eye peered through the gap. 'Oh, it's you Lewis, come in quickly.'

She opened the door wide enough for me to get in, then slammed it closed. Alone with her baby she looked distraught, confessing that she was at her wits' end with all the reporters and photographers tramping around the house. But after a few minutes she calmed down and we went into the nursery and saw this little creature lying in the cot, the face covered with a rash.

'What do you think Lewis, will the spots show in the picture?'

'It won't be a very pretty picture if I took it now,' I replied. 'I think we ought to wait until the rash clears up.'

Time and other commitments intervened and I never did take that picture of the baby, or any other picture of her as circumstances determined. Mary and Robert Shaw got married and I didn't see her again until the Elstree meeting.

I had finished my stint with Eastwood and now wanted to photograph Mary and get back to my studio. It was just before lunch and she had to have her hair done for a 'take' in the afternoon. I sat and watched the hairdresser working on it, sensing an uneasy atmosphere. Perhaps I was tired or mistaken, but I am sure that Mary's personality had changed during the intervening six years or so since our last meeting. In the Royal Court she was most considerate with all the people she worked with and everybody loved her, from the directors down to the stage hands. I had heard some mutterings from one or two of the people on the perimeter here but discounted it as the usual bitchiness that abounds in these areas.

When the hair had been put in curlers and a scarf tied around her head, she came over and sat next to me. I told her that I had done Clint and now it was her turn. 'Oh no, not with a scarf on my head. Can you wait until after lunch when the curlers are taken out?'

I reluctantly agreed although the pictures were not glamour shots but simply actors and actresses on location. The head scarf, if anything, would have added to that atmosphere, but she was adamant.

After lunch I watched a rehearsal in which she featured. Her whole manner seemed to say, 'Star!' It wasn't the Mary I had previously known; the warmth that used to surround her had disappeared. The rehearsals went on and on and the day was fast coming to an end. I had to get back to my studio as there was a deadline on the Eastwood picture, the main shot. Mary's was of secondary importance. I waited another hour with still no sign of a 'take'. The rehearsals were getting very tense so I decided to call it a day and went up to Mary, informing her that I was off, as I couldn't wait until her scarf was!

It was not a good experience but films generate different vibes to theatre and as I have never been totally comfortable with filming, I may have been generating my own bad vibes. In theatre I was in control. I read the play, worked out what I wanted to shoot and was fortunate enough to be one of the photographers who was allowed on stage. Quite often, photographers were required to shoot offstage, during rehearsals, which was hopeless because you couldn't get the shots you wanted.

I hated working on feature films and avoided that sort of work. One sat there like a nerd, until they shouted 'Stills!' and then one got up and clicked the camera. You could spend the whole day, lucky just to get two shots. You cannot shoot while they're shooting, because of the noise and you can't possibly get into the positions you want.

There is not the same *esprit de corps* on a film set. On stage everyone is working together. The actors do their own make-up and might only have a dresser as an additional person. In a film, the actors may play out all their scenes in isolation, never actually playing face to face with other cast members. And then there are all the other crew members to deal with, hair, make-up, costume etc. You might have 30 people reacting to your one piece of temperament.

One of the few films I worked on was Terence Young's *Serious Charge*, with Anthony Quayle and Cliff Richard in a small part. That was enough for me.

a blow-out…

Going to see films was a different matter. I had been an addict since childhood when I cut my teeth on the celluloid teething ring as I sat on my mother's knee during the family's weekly outing of feast and film . . . a 'blow-out' as we children called it. First, a restaurant visit where we were allowed to indulge ourselves without restraint, followed by attendance at the latest film at one of the local cinemas. It was a habit I continued with increasing self-indulgence, going to the cinema in Hounslow, when I was at art school, or Notting Hill Gate when I lived there. The suburban cinemas showed the same films as in London but at a much cheaper price and each suburb had its cinema, sometimes even two.

When we wanted foreign films we went to one of the cult cinemas, the Globe in Putney for Japanese films, the Academy Cinema in Oxford Street for French films. At the Hampstead Everyman they showed the things that nobody else would show, like *The Battleship Potemkin* and the Maxim Gorky Trilogy.

What amused me about these places was that in any lavatory in any ordinary cinema, you'd find four-letter words written on the walls, but if you went to the lavatory at the Hampstead Everyman, you'd most likely find a political slogan, or remarks like: 'Please don't throw your cigarettes into the lavatory. It makes them taste so bad!'

The thinking man's dunny.

brief encounters of the first kind...

My passion for films meant I was thrilled to meet one of the more innovative of the French directors. I can't remember who commissioned me, it may have been *She* magazine, or *Woman's Own*, but it really doesn't matter. What does matter is that the negatives of Francois Truffaut exist in my files and the slightly surreal meeting exists in my memory.

It was no mere chance that I had seen Truffaut's latest film *Jules and Jim* which I greatly admired and hoped to discuss with him. But the anticipated exchange did not eventuate, nor did any earth-shattering discourse on the subtler nuances of Hitchcockian influence on the New Wave of French Cinema. In reality, it was more like a short act from Marcel Marceau. (Curiously, when I photographed Marceau, mime was replaced by a voluble discourse, where we had a long, one-sided conversation in his highly accented English about how all of his mime creations must be put on film to preserve them for posterity.)

The simple reason for the lack of dialogue with Truffaut was that my familiarity with the Gallic tongue was, and still is, virtually non-existent and at that time, his English matched my French.

We met, as arranged, in the hotel foyer and I took the opportunity of grabbing a few shots there, making use of the large mirrors on the walls of the reception area. I suggested by hand signals and some very fractured Franglais that we should then '*continue dans la rue*'.

It was fairly chilly in the street outside and he put his collar up and extracted another cigarette from the crumpled blue packet of French fags. Then he lit it, cupping his hands to protect the flickering flame from the wind, hunching his shoulders as he inhaled. It was pure Bogart from a scene in any of his earlier gangster movies, metamorphosed, perhaps subconsciously, by Truffaut's mind.

Plaintive pleas, partly obliterated by a *mélange* of little white puffs of condensed breath issued from my mouth. '*Marchez, s'il vous plaît*, stop! *tournez, regardez moi.*'

From his mouth issued larger cumulus clouds, not so much frozen breath but smoke from the incessant Gauloises that he lit in an unbroken chain. In between the clicks of my camera and his lighter, I did manage to convey my admiration for *Jules and Jim* which to this day remains my favourite Truffaut. After a few more poses and lots more cigarettes I exposed my final shots and wound the film through.

'*Ça va, j'ai finis, merci, très beaucoup.*' We wended our way back to the hotel and I made my *au revoirs* to which he responded with a genial '*C'est un plaisir*'. It transformed the bleak afternoon into a spring day.

Blue Band...

Although I did not enjoy film work, I occasionally did television commercials. A series of these were for Tony Schaeffer and others for J. Walter Thompson.

One of the assignments involved shooting four commercials in two days for Blue Band margarine. There were a series of stills needed and some live action at the end. The whole film crew turned up for the still photographs, even though their section was minimal, so I told them to get it over with and go.

'We thought we'd do the lighting for you,' said one of the lighting chaps.

'Bring me a bank of floods,' I replied. 'I don't need any other lighting.'

There was unspoken amazement at this but they said nothing, and simply complied with my request. When the live action sequence was finished, the camera crew left but I noticed the lighting boys stayed behind, perhaps still thinking they'd be needed.

I put on the bank of flood lights and told the actors to go ahead with the script. Then, I shot the stills the way I would have shot front-of-house for the theatre, running about, shooting over the shoulder and so forth.

It was a frantic schedule but at the end of two days we had all the contacts marked off for blow-ups and twelve or fifteen prints ready a few days later, when they were needed. The commercial actually appeared on television the following week, which was record time.

Shortly after this, there was a knock at the door of my studio and there were the three lighting chaps. 'Can we come in?' they asked.

'Yes.'

'. . . come to apologise mate,' they continued.

'What for?' I asked.

'We thought you were a stupid prick, running about like that. All the other photographers have tripods, and there you were, like some mad bastard, snapping away with one set of lights. "It's going to be a proper balls-up," we said to ourselves, but we've seen the shots, and they're fantastic.'

That's the way I shot all my commercials, the usual time is two or three days, but I was generally finished in one. I have always worked quickly, partly to get through the thing, and partly to get over my anxiety about doing it.

there's a girl in my soup... again...

I was still doing theatre work and showbiz portraits but my sixties thing was coming to an end. The whole scene was becoming a little jaded for me, there was a new era coming in, change in the air. The sixties were over.

Theatre no longer played host to the sometimes raw, but exciting plays that had literally tumbled out over the last ten or fifteen years. Tastes and priorities had changed. The angry young men had tasted success and the leanness had been replaced by a visible layer of flab. Money mattered.

The plays that I was now photographing were productions like *Girl in My Soup* and revivals. Plays like *Little Malcolm and his Struggle Against the Eunuchs* had been thrown out with the bath water.

Not all the plays of the sixties were good. There was a lot of pretentious rubbish staged, but there were also a lot of plays. During my stint with the theatre, I took front-of-house photographs for over one hundred West End productions. Some ran for ages, some did not survive the first night. But regardless of their worth, a lot of actors read and performed them. They learnt them and learnt from them. There were many awful plays produced from texts that shouldn't have even merited a reading, and many awesome ones from new talent, fostered by the fecund climate.

Although I was travelling a lot, engaged with overseas assignments for advertising agencies and destination photography for travel agents, I was aware that much of the excitement of the early days had vanished. The disregard for accepted photographic conventions that one had indulged in, the experimentations and fun that were an integral part of every job one tackled, were no longer present. The joy had gone out of photography. I had never taken it seriously, although I did apply myself seriously to the jobs I was given. Now, I was beginning to feel a certain dissatisfaction with what I was doing. The compressed energy that once accompanied every job, regardless of subject, was absent.

There was now a nagging ennui beneath the once apparent surface enthusiasm.

When I told the chief art buyer for one of the advertising agencies for whom I worked that I was emigrating to Australia, she was surprised and tried her best to dissuade me. 'I know the industry is going through a thin time,' she reasoned, 'but we have been feeding you with plenty of work and will continue to do so, as long as you want it.'

I didn't want it and I couldn't explain why. I didn't know myself at the time. All I knew was that I wanted to start afresh in a new location. My career, which had been conceived in the fifties, was born in the sixties. The umbilicus had been cut but my adherence to it was so close as to be almost incestuous. The sixties, which I had loved, was dead. I, too, had to depart.

Among my last theatrical jobs were two disparate productions which seemed to sum up, for me at least, the state of theatre at that time. One was *The Council of Love*, a nineteenth-century play, rewritten by John Bird. It had been banned during its premiere production and its author charged with blasphemy. The orgy scenes which I photographed for front-of-house displayed bare breasts, and other controversial scenes included God, Jesus and the Virgin Mary. I believe this was the first time such revealing photographs had been displayed outside a legitimate West End theatre. This production, like its predecessor, was also charged with blasphemy, with some suggesting that the charge was a publicity stunt, concocted by the producers. It fizzled, confirming the public's jaded attitude towards morality, especially where it pertained to religion. Tedium, rather than *Te Deum*. The seemingly trumped-up charge wasn't taken up by the Press and no public outcry accompanied the whimper that went out with this over-ambitious effort.

The sets depicted Heaven, Hell and the Vatican. The costumes that went with them could have paid a Pope's ransom but the enormous cast, including Lally Bowers and Warren Mitchell, was, according to some sources, never adequately reimbursed for their services.

The other play was *Girl in My Soup*—AGAIN!!! It had first opened in 1966 and four years later it was still playing to full houses. I photographed most of Michael Codron's productions and he always asked me for my opinion as to whether it would run or not. I seemed to hit on the right answer more often than not and remember saying that though I thought *Little Malcolm...* was terrific and the actors, superb, it wouldn't run. It didn't. When I first photographed *Girl in My Soup* I expressed my opinion. I disliked the play, but it would run. Run it did. As one of the last theatre jobs before I left England, I felt it was an omen. I was, in a way, repeating myself, without any fault or control of my own. I had now photographed the play seven times. Only *Billy Liar* exceeded that total, with eight reshootings in all.

behind the fridge...

Just a few months before emigrating I was working on a book with Peter Cook and Dudley Moore, entitled *The Dagenham Papers*. 'We'll see you in Australia then,' said Peter. 'We're doing an Australian tour, first stop, Sydney. It's to be called *Behind the Fridge*'.

I photographed Pete and Dud posing behind an open fridge door in Peter's Hampstead house, along with several other situations for the forthcoming Australian production.

It was only a matter of weeks after our arrival in Australia that Pete and Dud followed. At this time, my family and I were still settling in and were staying *pro tem*, with our old friends from England, the Hayes. We were ensconced in their beautiful stone cottage in Hunters Hill, a select area which boasted a few remaining houses that had been built in the earliest period of Sydney's settlement. It was arranged that Pete and Dud would have dinner with us, a relaxed quiet evening. 'Do you know,' said Peter, 'it's ten years since *The Fringe*? We've all changed, haven't we?'

It wasn't till then that I realised we had. On my side, I had changed not only habitat, but country. I had uprooted my wife, son and father-in-law and left behind relatives, friends, a large, comfortable house in Richmond, a West End studio and an established reputation. Now, I had to start from scratch in a completely new environment.

Pete and Dud had also gone through a metamorphosis, which to this day is still unresolved. Their rise from undergrad footlighters to club owners and entertainers, to Hollywood stars, incorporated changes that were not only economic but professional, and perhaps what was most significant, their domestic partnerships.

Here was Pete with Judy Huxtable, soon to be the new Mrs Cook. Dudley was still married to Suzy Kendall, who was working in Los Angeles. He told me that Suzy was lucky to be alive, having been invited to the fateful Sharon Tate party, and for some reason, unable to attend.

A lot of water had flowed under the bridge since *The Fringe* days. Jonathon Miller had gone into directing films and operas, but had kept his medical interests alive. Later he produced the very successful, *The Body in Question.* Alan Bennett was a successful playwright while Pete and Dud had gone on to television and films. There seemed to be no end to the boys' fortune... wasn't it The Fortune Theatre where they established themselves?

That night Dud and I were discussing John Betjeman and I showed him the poem Betjeman had written for me. Printed on the broadsheet was another poem, 'The Crem' which brought tears to his eyes. Peter had left the dinner table by now and was sitting cross-legged in the garden, surrounded by the notorious Hunters Hill mosquitoes. He was slapping away left, right and centre and repeating in a low monotone, 'Things have changed, things have changed...'

The other guests were a little puzzled. Why weren't they being funny? Where were the excruciating Pete and Dud dialogues? Earlier in the evening, during the dessert, Dud had brought the house down by just saying, 'Bum!' several times in varying tones.

All conversation had ceased. The only sounds were the whirring of the mozzies, homing in. Peter's litany of change, punctuated by slaps to his exposed flesh, were interrupted by the occasional, almost inaudible sob from Dudley.

As I write this, I think back and realise that Sean Kenny is no longer with us and Pete and Dud no longer exist as a double act, except on vinyl or acetate. Dudley has made it big in Glitter City, while Pete's career has been chequered and less easy to define. I suppose we have all changed. We have gone a little beyond the fringe and there's no turning back.

TERRA AUSTRALIS

Australia...

In Australia, as in the United Kingdom, my photographic assignments were mixed. In the very beginning I was engaged in both advertising and magazine photography, working from the studio of a Swedish photographer who was one of Australia's leading food photographers.

We had come to the new country at the continual cajoling of Babette Hayes, a longstanding friend in England, who had made the quantum leap herself a few years earlier. We were periodically awakened in the early hours of the morning by phone calls, where a chirpy voice would extol the virtues of the lucky country, the weather, food and lifestyle. 'Come out and join us,' was always the closing plea, 'you'll love it here.'

We had resisted these pleas for a number of years and it wasn't until the start of the new decade that the idea of joining the Hayes was even remotely entertained.

By 1970 we were comfortably settled in a large house in Richmond and I was still busy workwise, although the signs of a slump in the industry were becoming more obvious. Also becoming more obvious was my growing dissatisfaction with the direction I had been following.

The realisation that I was moving in ever-decreasing circles and would end up following the flight of the Whooslum bird, made the 10,000 mile journey to Australia more desirable. It was a country I was not totally unfamiliar with, having spent a brief holiday with my parents there in 1941, before returning to Hong Kong to await the pleasure of being entertained by Emperor Hirohito for the next four years.

In England I watched a lot of photographers going down the gurgler, while others, with the capital and know-how, either diversified or got out of the profession altogether. How long could I keep my balance? The continued entreaties from Australia began to undermine my resistance.

If things didn't go well in the new country, I would have enough assets to return to England and face up to what might have confronted me in the first place. But things did go well and we are still here after 21 years. As luck would have it, I was presented with the key to the door on my arrival in Sydney and did not have to wait till now to receive it.

If Australia is still considered by some Europeans as a penal settlement then the time I have served to date has been in no way hard labour. More a labour of love, and I am looking forward, now that I have retired, to a life sentence without parole.

not in Japan...

Within a few weeks of our arrival in Australia, I was working as a freelance photographer from the studio of Ben Eriksson.

Pol magazine commissioned me to photograph Helen Glad, the grand-daughter of Australian artist, Norman Lindsay, whose buxom nymphs and satyrs had bounded across many thousands of illustrations, paintings and etchings during his long career.

During the course of photographing Helen, I remarked that she, being a female descendant of the most famous Australian painter of the nude, must be fed up with requests from photographers to shoot her in the nude. She informed me that she was prepared to be photographed in the nude, but only if certain conditions applied, conditions which no other photographer had, so far, been able to meet.

'What are the conditions?' I asked.

'Full frontal nudity, pubic hairs and all!' she stated.

'Right!' I said. 'You're on!'

I immediately phoned the editor of *Pol*, Maggie Mcqueeg.

'Maggie,' I said. 'I've shot some pics of Helen, but how would you like a nude?'

'Can you do it?' she replied, with a hint of disbelief.

'Yes, but there are conditions.'

'What?' asked Maggie, guardedly.

'You'll have to publish it full frontal, pubic hairs and all,' I stipulated, confirming Helen's prerequisite, as she stood next to me by the phone.

'Agreed!' said Maggie.

I made arrangements for Helen to come to the studio where I could set up the photograph.

I shot two positions. One with Lindsay's etchings projected onto the seated Helen. The other, which both Helen and I preferred, of Helen lying on her side with a full colour painting spread over her white flesh. The pubic area was only apparent as a black triangle which merged into the painting, most discreet and only discerned if carefully scrutinised. I had kept to the conditions without having a blatant, confrontational image. Helen was satisfied with the results.

I discussed the photographs with Maggie and it was decided that the full colour shot would be used, but when the article appeared it was accompanied by the etching photograph, which was cropped to include only the upper part of the body. I was livid and felt that Helen would think I had cheated by getting her to pose and then going back on my word.

Maggie was apologetic. The magazine was printed in Japan and although the pubic hairs were virtually indiscernible, the Japanese quality control, preparing the transparency for platemaking, would have revealed them, resulting in automatic censorship because of the Japanese obsession with eliminating every trace of pubic hirsuteness for public observation.

Here was an enigma to ponder over regarding the complexities and twisted logic of cultural taboos.

The country that had created some of the world's most explicit art and outrageous pornography, relishing in the portrayal of larger than life-size genitalia, shys away from the depiction of a few actual pubic hairs.

Belle...

Belle was one of the magazines that I freelanced for in Australia and Babette Hayes, the designer with whom I most frequently worked. Early in our association we were in Germany, on behalf of the German Tourist Board, to photograph some commercial establishments and specific architectural subjects. Whilst there, Babette thought it a good idea to include some domestic lifestyles and telephoned the editor of *Schonne Wohnen.*

The editor, who had never heard of *Belle* and held a poor opinion of Australia's contribution to the world of interiors, was inclined to give us the brush-off. This created a temperature rise in Babette's French blood and some heated words, followed by a cool exchange of opinions, led to a reluctant invitation to the offices of *Schonne Wohnen.* I was rather embarrassed and wanted to forget the meeting but Babette was made of sterner stuff and we fronted up a little later, with a couple of copies of *Belle* clutched in my sweaty hands.

After a short wait in the vast glass and chrome Stern building, which incorporated *Schonne Wohnen*, we were taken to meet the editor, a rather formidable lady, who did not smile as we introduced ourselves. She asked us to be seated but kept standing herself and without a pause said that she was sorry but there was nothing much she could do for us. Her English was good but devoid of emotion.

She asked to see the magazines I was clutching and relieved me of them by taking them between her thumb and forefinger, as though they were contaminated. She started to flick through, then hesitated on a page and turned back to the beginning, this time going through the book with careful deliberation. Finally she looked up from the article which had caught her attention. 'This is you,' she said, pointing her finger at us and wagging it like a horizontal metronome. The article was credited, so our names had registered, in spite of the apparent lack of interest shown during the introduction. She sat down and for the first time, smiled. 'Have you time for lunch? We can eat in the restaurant downstairs.'

The massive dining room was, in reality, a canteen for the hundreds of staff who occupied the building. It was like an airship hangar, with globular lights, and tables topped with vitreous enamel. Blue and red op art designs crisscrossed and scored the surface.

Madame Editor was very impressed and very surprised that a magazine of *Belle*'s quality had come out of a place like Australia. In the event, she couldn't do enough for us, supplying names and addresses of houses that would be interesting to photograph and details of architects who could be of use. We parted on good terms which were put to further use on subsequent visits to Germany.

Our German visits included stays at the Four Seasons Hotel in Munich and The Atlantic in Hamburg. In London, it was the Savoy, places I could never have afforded, but which as a photographer for a prestige magazine, I now had access to.

the Westminister [*sic*] system...

What London does today, Sydney does a bit later and it wasn't long before Australian politics got in on the act with its own version of the Keeler scandal.

The whole mess which embroiled the Labor Party in Australia was a local drama company's bedroom farce compared to the Tories' widescreen blockbuster, shot, in more ways than one, on a stage that included diverse locations—a love nest in Bayswater, a Nash house in Regent's Park, a cabaret club and strip joint, foreign embassies and the swimming pool of a country house.

The cast was as varied and bizarre as the locations. Millionaire prostitutes, property dealers, MI5 agents, West Indians, a gun-toting lover, a prime minister and an osteopath/artist who manipulated more than mere bones.

When I arrived in Australia at the beginning of the 1970s, I was lucky to land on my feet and immediately immerse myself in the emergence of what turned out to be the Australian version of the sixties.

It was a softer replay, an echo of the previous ten years in the UK from which I had just extricated myself. Ironically, the Australians have a certain contempt for their New Zealand neighbours and accuse *them* of being behind the times. 'You have just landed in Wellington, please put your clocks back ten years.' Without wishing to give offence, I must admit that this old adage applied perfectly to Sydney in 1971.

I left behind a surfeit of photographs of the nude, in nearly every aspect of photography, both commercial and private. Even the theatre got in on the act with *Hair*, *Oh Calcutta* and *The Council of Love*.

Not only did Antipodean entertainment, fashion and lifestyle strive to mirror the past, it caught up with a market devoid of goods but overflowing with eager consumers, ready to devour every nuance of the swinging sixties. Even politics got in on the act.

In 1961 I had photographed Christine Keeler, whose doings had threatened to bring down the entire British political machine. A decade later, in Australia, I was approached to photograph a woman who had been linked to a politician, and a scandal had erupted which threatened the future of the party involved.

I was contacted by the editor of one of the magazines I was freelancing for and asked to her office to meet the lady. It was specified that I was to photograph her in my studio. There were studios in the building where the magazine was housed and a whole scad of photographers on staff who could have taken the picture. Why had I been chosen for the job? No one knew of my connection to the Keeler photograph then.

Despite the similar circumstances, the differences between Junie Morosi and Christine Keeler were paramount. I found Keeler a pleasant enough person but she did not send the blood coursing through my veins. Any excitement generated was journalistic rather than sexual. Morosi was an entirely different matter, poised, intelligent and beautiful.

In my studio, before the session, I discovered that she spoke Cantonese and we spent some time in light-hearted Chinese chit-chat before commencing work.

Some people exude an electrical charge, a kind of aura. It might be a benign experience, it might be positively negative or hostile but with Morosi, it hummed with a suppressed energy, held in perfect control. She supplied a spark to any conversation, investing words which would sound banal from someone else, with an intensity that gave them significance. I was bowled over by her personality and in all my years of meeting and photographing personalities, I can only recall a dozen or so times that this phenomenon occurred.

I shot the required pictures in colour and when the lady journalist, who had been with us throughout the shoot, left, I shot off a couple of rolls in black and white. I still find these latter images more revealing than the coloured ones used for the cover of the magazine.

Lloyd Rees...

It was my first visit to Lloyd Rees, the grand old man of Australian art. I was there to take some pictures to illustrate an article for a fashion magazine. It was a double feature, so to speak, for I was also to photograph another ancient artist, two national treasures preserved on one film.

After a preliminary interview and photo session, Lloyd Rees had to make his way with us to the home of Desiderius Orban, who was celebrating his 99th birthday. Rees, a mere 88, and a youngster in comparison, was deemed to be Mohammed. He went to the mountain, and the mountain was no longer firm as a rock, and could not for physical, as opposed to spiritual reasons, go to him.

If life is considered to be a lottery then the two artists, on this occasion, 88 and 99 respectively, were the winning numbers. They shared 187 years, failing sight, shakey pins and unlimited enthusiasm. They embraced each other on meeting, and as with older men, kept their headgear firmly on their heads. Lloyd Rees was wearing his outdoor model, a black French beret, while Orban sported a Kangol-style cap, with thick-lensed, horn-rimmed glasses, with movable dark shades, looming from under its short peak.

Orban had made his way across the room to Rees aided by a stout cane, a support not needed by the junior member of the duo. Both were cheerful and laughter filled the studio. Then the relative quiet was shattered by the explosion of a champagne cork, flying out of the mouth of the bottle and hitting the ceiling with a resounding crack. It was the necessary prelude to the salutary toasting of the birthday, the bubbly liquid no less lively and effervescent than the celebrants themselves. A good vintage surpassed by two much rarer ones.

On this first visit at the Rees' home, the journalist and I had been introduced to Marjory Rees, who in no time had served us with a cup of tea. The gentle air of activity generated by this couple seemed to fill the otherwise empty house with a gentle hum of contented domesticity. There was an intimacy that surrounded them that seemed to bind them very close to each other.

This sensation was absent on my next visit to the house. It was a different journalist and without the buzz of anticipation of Orban's birthday. Then, everything had been in top gear and I didn't have the opportunity to do much else than take photos and generally avoid getting in the way of the slow-motion haste that filled the day.

This time the house seemed to be in shadow. The pink walls that had previously shone through the lush vegetation were a muted violet, no doubt due to the day, rather than the mood which continued within the four walls themselves. Now there was only Rees, his wife having succumbed to a debilitating illness that left him, more or less to himself.

We reacquainted ourselves and this time there was less bustle and hurry. I had the opportunity of taking many more photographs and having a real conversation rather than just the niceties that filled in the gaps in dialogue of our previous meeting.

The photographs from the initial session had contained some shots of Rees laughing and I was subsequently contacted by his son in Tasmania to request permission to use the image on a poster for an exhibition to be held there. It was, he said, the only photograph he had seen of his father laughing.

One should not be misled by this remark for Rees was cheerful and enthusiastic, his earnestness perhaps taking the place of the inane smiles that so many of us use as a surface decoration, to mask our real feelings. His real feelings were covered only by a cloak of hospitality and a generous giving of his precious time. His wife's illness affected him profoundly but he did not wallow in self-pity and unload his grief on visitors.

During the photographic session he donned his paint-peppered, khaki working smock and his inevitable straw hat. We spoke, when I had him to myself, about artists both past and present, his time in Europe, and of course the hype that surrounded his late work, thin washes of colour that formed abstracted landscapes.

I asked him what he thought of the media's comparison of his work with that of the English master, Turner. 'Of course,' he replied, 'one admires Turner, but I am not consciously imitating him. It's my eyes. I cannot see too well these days and I use the colour to feel the shape.'

The adulation of his work and the high prices had been long delayed in their arrival and although flattered by the public's acclaim at this late stage of his career, he regretted that it hadn't happened earlier, when full use could have been made of it. But if there was any bitterness it was not apparent. His gratitude at the vagaries of fame during these twilight years outweighed any other feelings that lesser men might have succumbed to.

I photographed him in his studio, from the outside, through the large glass window, splattered with paint, that covered one entire wall of the studio. The spots of paint that had flown from his brushes in countless encounters with the blank canvas, had transformed certain sections into a pointillistic echo of Seurat.

Segal, the American artist, who encases his subjects in plaster of Paris, came into my mind when I was confronted with the sink in the studio. The sink, and the whole surrounding area had been covered with a coating of plaster of Paris and paint, over the years of frantic activity. It had metamorphosed into a three-dimensional still life which retained a vestige of animation in the tap that continued to work in spite of its encrusted surface.

There are certain photographs that I have taken which I attach more importance to than others, not because they are particularly good photographs—in fact some of my favourites are pretty poor examples of the photographic art—but because of the situation or the person involved, which becomes bound to the image. Lloyd Rees is a case in point. I hold the photographs I have of him as rather special. They reveal, I think, more than just the man who created the two dimensional images on various surfaces for the world to see. He had an art of greater depth that lay hidden, but often exposed itself. It was the art of humanism and I feel fortunate to have shared a few moments with him, which I can relive when I come across the prints I have made.

Renishaw visited...

Paradoxically, after I had settled in Australia, one of my overseas assignments was the UK and the subject, country houses. Betsy, the journalist I was working with, was an American and as she showed me the list of houses to be featured, I said in mock grief, 'What! No Renishaw! I was hoping there'd be Renishaw.'

She looked at me, puzzled. 'Why do you say that? There was quite a long list of houses and that name was included... I left it out, but if you want to go there...?' So Renishaw, country home of the Sitwell family, situated in Derbyshire, became the third house on our list.

We'd been staying two or three nights at each of the houses, depending on the amount of work to be done, but the days couldn't pass quickly enough for me, waiting to keep the rendezvous which had been at the back of my mind all these years. A rendezvous which I'd felt I never had any hope of realising. Now, here it was, only a few hours away.

We arrived there in the late afternoon, expecting to be met by Reresby Sitwell, Osbert's nephew, and the new owner of the house. The door at the front was ajar and when we tentatively knocked, no one appeared. Peeking cautiously around it, we were confronted by two, life-size eighteenth-century wooden figures. They were holding halberds but something wasn't quite right. On closer inspection, the figure on the left had a pair of horn-rimmed glasses perched on his nose. It was incongruous and it lent the house a feeling of relaxation and easygoing humour, soon confirmed when our view was blocked by a large figure wearing a Harris tweed jacket with elbow patches. It was Reresby Sitwell, very much the country gent, exuding geniality. He welcomed us with a smile and warmth which rivalled the blazing log fire in the open hearth. It was flanked by a mural, painted on canvas panels, which had been commissioned by Sir Osbert from John Piper, as were the watercolour sketches of the Castello Montegufoni that I had photographed in the bedroom of his York House flat, twenty years before.

Drinks were offered but I opted for tea as did Penelope, Reresby's wife, who had now joined us. I needed thawing out. The long drive had left me a little creaky. It was cold outside and the house was warm, in a way we were to remember with nostalgic longing in the days that followed. Some of the other houses had all the assets of good food, wines, comfortable beds and the host's amity, but were hard to warm to when the window panes were encrusted with arabesques of feathery frost and the floor of the bedroom was a vast ocean of marble with only the tiniest islands of scatter rugs.

The fate of Renishaw had been precarious. The feeling had been that on Osbert's demise the death duties would be so horrendous that Montegufoni (which Sacheverelle, the younger brother hoped to inherit) would have to be sold. Being the only brother it was certain that he would inherit the baronial title, as Osbert was childless, but the uncertainties relating to the land and property caused bitter disappointment and wrangling, before and after Osbert's death.

Fortunately for Reresby, Osbert had made up his mind that he would retire to Montegufoni and leave Renishaw in the capable hands of his nephew, which Reresby had resolved to restore to all its former glory. The money needed was substantial so he resorted to that great institution for impoverished gentry, paying guests. Renishaw was added to the list of Historic Houses that catered for a well-heeled public who wanted to spend a few days in an environment normally inaccessible to them. Wining and dining at the same table, and at times actually being served by a Knight of the Realm, a Lord of the Manor, or a Baron. Needless to say the bulk of these paying guests were Americans and quite a few (pre-recession) Australians.

Reresby had been an account executive at Colman, Prentis and Varley, the advertising agency I'd worked for when I finished my art school training. So our table talk was a long reminiscence of the agency days, our mutual acquaintances and memories of the awful characters who worked there. We also spoke of Sir Osbert, but the subject of David Horner was skirted around. He was interested in the photographs I had taken of his uncle and I promised I would send some if I could find the negatives.

We spent two days and nights there, Betsy trying all the time to interview Reresby. She was hoping for a meaningful 'in-depth' profile, but Reresby's recitation of the history of Renishaw, delivered in the manner of Raymond Massey as a bearded Abraham Lincoln declaiming the Gettysburg Address, took up most of the time. I was busy photographing the garden and the stables, the folly and the house itself. The famous Sargent family portrait that I knew only from reproduction was now in front of me in paint, as opposed to print, and I reacquainted myself with all the subjects I had previously photographed in York House, during the final days of the legendary trio, Osbert, Edith and Sacheverelle.

At Renishaw it was hunt the thimble, only to find a complete haberdashery. What a reward! Everything comes to him who waits.

prelude...

On one of my frequent visits to the UK I happened to have some portraits which I had brought with me to show a photographic colleague. When he saw them he suggested that the National Portrait Gallery might be interested in them.

I had never considered them meritorious, in spite of the fact that my ego insisted that they were a lot better than some of the meretricious published images I had seen of the same people. So two days before I was due to fly back, I contacted the Gallery and spoke to the Curator of Photography. I explained that I had a few photos of Aneurin Bevan, Somerset Maugham, Osbert Sitwell and Cecil Beaton that he might be interested in. He was and invited me to come around at once. I took my courage in both hands and my feet to the National Portrait Gallery photographic division.

Colin Ford, the Curator, explained that the Gallery had a limited budget of around £9 per photo, concluding that he would be very interested in the photos if I would accept their current rate. He was quite surprised when I said that I wouldn't. They could have them gratis. I didn't need the money and was more than pleased that they had offered to buy them. This was the start of the Lewis Morley Archive at the National Portrait Gallery and also the start of my fantasy of having an exhibition there.

I have had several exhibitions, both photographic and mixed media; painting, assemblage and sculpture. These I took as a matter of course, but the wish for this seemingly impossible fantasy to materialise, occasionally surfaced when I saw an exhibition there. I would immediately put it out of my mind however, not wanting to waste time and energy pursuing a chimera. It was like my childhood fantasy of marrying Alice Faye, the unrealisable, impossible dream.

Each year, on my European assignments, I visited the National Portrait Gallery, and let them have a photo or two that I had unearthed from the mound of 1960s portraits I had taken.

realisation...

Working in Australia brought me into contact with another old friend, Maggie Eckhardt, who had come back to her home country after a successful career in modelling and entered the realms of interior design.

We collaborated once more, but not as photographer and model. Instead I photographed some of the interiors she had designed. It led to other assignments together, travelling interstate, to the Solomon Islands and the United Kingdom.

It was during one of these trips, in 1987, that the National Portrait Gallery told me they would give me an exhibition in two years' time. Here was the catalyst that led to the realisation of a vague ambition that had been forming in my mind—the desire to retire from active photography and devote myself to cataloguing and printing the thousands of negatives which I had never had time to consider seriously.

Fate, which had not to date deserted me, kept dealing me hands liberally sprinked with aces, but I knew that to exhibit for The National Portrait Gallery show I would have to devote the intervening two years solely to its preparation.

There were misgivings. How was I going to support myself for two years without working? Once again fate smiled and bestowed her blessings on me, far beyond my expectations.

Prior to my trip to the UK there had been tentative enquiries about my studio in Sydney, which was situated at the back of a hotel, built after I first moved into the premises. I hated the vast brick cube that now loomed over me, with its hideous windows, like the myriad facets of a fly's eyes, constantly peering down into my backyard.

The owners of the hotel, a powerful conglomerate, had been playing cat and mouse with me, buying out my next-door neighbour, then offering to buy me out. The offer was renewed, reneged on, renewed, until finally, out of exasperation, I named a price, out of pique and out of proportion, expecting another protracted wrangle. To my surprise, they accepted. The sale enabled me to give up active commercial photography and pursue the now realised fantasy of financial independence.

dream...

My exhibition at The National Portrait Gallery was an unexpected but welcome accolade that came at the right time. Originally it was conceived as a retrospective, but as the moment of decision drew closer, it was oriented to a sixties theme, and 'Lewis Morley—Photographer of the Sixties' was decided upon.

By some further quirk of fate, publicity for the exhibition and publicity for another sixties phenomenon, the Keeler Affair, as represented in the film *Scandal*, coincided. Together they gave birth to an image that publicised both the film, where Joanna Whalley as Keeler recreated the pose, and my soon to follow exhibition, publicised by the original photograph itself.

The opening night of the exhibition witnessed a further, more anticipated juxtaposition, as many of the people featured in the photographs turned up to gaze at their earlier images, hoping perhaps that they mirrored the contemporary ones. They didn't, the one of myself included.

In my own self-portrait I saw a smug photographer, holding the inevitable cigarette, seated in front of a large blow-up of *The Fringe* boys. Catching my reflection in the glass on the frame I saw a much older and not particularly wiser person, but such sobering thoughts were banished in the far greater happiness I felt at seeing the realisation of a dream.

As was to be expected, many of those pictured could not turn up on the opening night. Albert Finney was only a few yards away from the venue but could not come as he was on stage with his own show. Others were too far away to come or absent for that most undisputed of excuses—The Grim Reaper.

A welcome, though uninvited guest suddenly appeared in the form of Koo Stark, and just as suddenly disappeared. The star of the show, so to speak, Christine Keeler, had requested eleven invitations but did not materialise with even one. Perhaps we will meet again one day and I will get an answer to many of the questions that have puzzled me in the intervening years.

the Christian syndrome...

As far back as I can remember, I have been very conscious of feeling guilt for various deeds perpetrated, both intentionally and unintentionally. What is more, I sometimes feel guilty for other people's crimes! This is not to say that I have perpetually been down in the mouth and unable to enjoy life. In fact, I have had a very active and often selfish, self-indulgent existence, satisfying my desires without too much regard for others' feelings or the consequences. But I was cursed with 'the Christian syndrome'.

This was not directly related to the teachings of Christ but with the character of Christian, from John Bunyan's *Pilgrim's Progress*. Among my father's fairly catholic library, where among the standard literature there was a fair share of radical publications, there was an illustrated edition of *The Pilgrim's Progress*.

The sombre black and white pictures depicted a stooped man, going through various episodes in his life, carrying a large bundle lashed to his back which represented his accumulated sins. For some reason, I associated myself closely with this figure. I remember, during my formative sexual years, in the midst of some innocuous depravity, the act of pulling up my playmate's skirt to have a look at her knickers, for instance, would be prematurely aborted when the vision of that stooped man materialised before my eyes.

Christian's appearance was an occurrence that plagued me throughout my life. As I grew older, the bundle, still attached, would fluctuate, matching its size with my years and misdeeds. But I devised a way of controlling its growth, a sort of mental chemotherapy. If the bundle had grown because of some task left undone, a little bit of it would drop off when I finally managed to discharge it. With maturity, Christian would still make his unwelcome visits but less frequently, and if his bundle had diminished somewhat, this was perhaps due to my coarsening conscience.

He materialised unexpectedly one day at the sight of a slightly stooped figure in a white suit, white Panama hat and brown and white correspondent's shoes. It was in the lounge of a hotel in Famagusta, where I had just finished the day's shooting of a holiday brochure for a London travel firm. The figure, hesitating momentarily in his slight shamble, was Barry Humphries.

guilt off the gingerbread...

It had all started the day he came to my studio to have his photograph taken for display in the foyer of The Establishment downstairs. He was due to appear in a one-man revue at the club's miniscule theatre. Unfortunately, the reception of his London debut was of similar proportions.

There was a slight battle of wills. Barry knew what he wanted and I knew what I wanted. After several coffees and too many cigarettes on my part, we came to a compromise. The results suited the theatre and they must have suited

Barry too as he commissioned me to photograph him in his apartment in Little Venice. Once again we each had our own ideas of how things should proceed but this time it was more of a collaboration than a compromise and some useful pictures resulted.

We photographed outside the apartment by the canal and in front of the entrance, by the railings or any suitable background that suited the mood. But it was the apartment itself that fascinated and stunned me. I had never seen, in one fell swoop, so many Charles Condors, their fan-shapes clinging to the walls like bats in a crowded cave.

As well, there were paintings, prints, watercolours, Art Nouveau *objets d'art*, Victorian screens, Ormolu clocks, ornate candlesticks and figures in gilt and bronze. Ceramic Art Deco ladies peeped from under the wide rims of their picture hats to survey the opulence.

I visited the cave again with the prints Barry had chosen and now that there wasn't the pressing urgency of taking pictures, we spent a little time discussing the art scattered around the room.

Being a failed painter, my talk naturally turned to the subject of art. Barry, as well as his theatrical talent, was a painter in his own right and an authority on Charles Condor. After a long discourse on the subject, he went into another room and returned with a lithograph by Condor which he presented to me. I was overwhelmed by a most unexpected but greatly appreciated gift. As a fellow collector, a fascination for prints was one of the more obsessive facets of my personality and the compelling cause of my weekend visits to Portobello Market in search of treasures. Enter Christian, in disguise.

I had recently bought some C.R.W. Nevinson prints for an absurdly low price from an enigmatic dealer at the Portobello Market. There had been a couple of duplicate pulls, though in different states and I had been ecstatic.

When Barry gave me the Condor print, I told him I had just bought some Nevinsons for next to nothing.

'Nevinson!' he said in awe. 'Now, there's an artist. Very underrated, but superb. What a find!'

I detected a faint note of envy in his voice. 'Do you like Nevinson?' I asked.

'Very much,' he replied.

'I'll tell you what,' I continued. 'I have a couple of duplicate pulls, if you like you can have one.'

'No Lewis, you don't have to, really.'

'I'll get it round to you . . .'

And this was Christian's first appearance with regard to Barry, to be succeeded by several encores during a twenty-year saga.

Cyprus . . . eight years later . . .

'Jeeze, what the hell are you doing here?' said the white-suited figure.

'The usual rubbish,' I replied. 'What about you?'

'Relaxing for a couple of days,' said Barry, waving vaguely in the direction of the reception desk where his companion was engrossed in the frustrations of booking in.

A couple of days after Barry's arrival, I gave the models connected with my assignment a break and took a day off. I went for a drive around the island with Barry and crammed into a few hours what would have taken days for most tourists. There were encounters with camels, local gentry in mountain pubs and Salamis, where Barry fooled around in the ruins and posed with the antique statues. He declaimed from the pedestal in front of the stage and ran along the top tiers of stone seating in the amphitheatre at Kyrenia. It was exhausting but I took some memorable pictures.

The subject of Nevinson did not come up, either because Barry had forgotten it, or was too polite to mention it. On my part, I was waiting for a suitable opportunity to express my regrets for the unfulfilled offer, but it never arose.

Australia... 1972...

I had settled in and had started my own studio. Things were progressing well until dear Christian loomed up again when I read an advertisement for a forthcoming tour of Barry Humphries. Sydney was on the agenda and I knew I would have to do three things. One, find the Nevinson print that I had promised. Two, go and see the show. Three, go backstage, present the print and shed a little of the bundle.

Two, I went to see the show, three, I went backstage with family and friends but didn't present him with the Nevinson, or mention it because... one, I couldn't find it.

When I emigrated to Australia with my family, we flew out, while our goods and chattels followed at a more leisurely pace, by sea, in a container. The smaller items were stored in tea chests and until this day, over twenty years later, I still haven't unpacked all of them. In the earlier years of settling in, only a few of the chests had been tackled and unpacked.

Years later, on yet another tour, I was phoned by Barry's stage manager, Bill Passmore, coincidentally a colleague from The Establishment days, a former assistant to Sean Kenny.

'Did those pictures you took of Barry in Cyprus ever come out?' he asked. 'Barry mentioned them but he says he's never seen them.'

Re-enter Christian, staggering under the additional weight. But the awful truth had to be faced. The negatives were stored in some receptacle which I hadn't, as yet, identified.

resurrection...

It wasn't until I was preparing for the National Portrait Gallery exhibition that I really started to get myself together to excavate the mountain of negatives lying dead the last two decades.

When I did start, it was rather like a Stanley Spencer painting of *The Resurrection*. Torn, oblong white envelopes spewed out negatives in a cascade of forgotten faces and places, to be entered into identifying columns on the word processor—an electronic Book of Judgment—reindexing suitable images for salvation, echoing the painting's upturned tombstones and surging figures. I supposed that this blitz on the mounting heap of negatives was my own version of Lazarus' resurrection from the 'negcropolis'.

Cut to 1989, when I am in London with mixed feelings about the opening of my exhibition at the National Portrait Gallery. There was excitement that I was to participate in the Warholian 'fifteen minutes of fame' but this was tempered by the sobering thought that I was to partake of the spoils of success alone. The one person I wanted to be with me at this, the apex of my career, was my wife, but she had to remain in Australia with her father, whose eyesight had rapidly deteriorated.

A message was passed to me from the public relations people that Barry Humphries was trying to contact me and would I phone him. My pleasure in meeting up with an old chum was marred by the image of Christian, who once more hove into view.

When I contacted Barry, he invited me to dinner, to which I arrived with the exhibition catalogue, featuring a photograph of him in Little Venice, surrounded by his Condors.

He showed it to his wife, Liz Spender, and sadly explained that owing to recent legal obligations, they were no longer in his possession. He brightened up when I showed him some prints of the Cyprus session and asked if he could make use of them in a forthcoming program, 'The South Bank Show'.

'Barry,' I said, 'I owe you a Nevinson.' He appeared truly puzzled so I refreshed his memory and promised that at our next meeting, by hook or by crook, I would deliver it to him.

A further eighteen months were to pass before that time, then an unexpected phone call announced he was making a lightning visit to Australia to tie up a few loose ends and to see his two young children.

He arrived to take us out to dinner but once again I did not have the elusive Nevinson. However, he saw a lot of the photographs I had taken of him since our first meeting at The Establishment and expressed the wish that he could see all of them. He was returning within a few months to tour with his Sandy Stone character and perhaps he could see the contacts.

Firm dates had been fixed for the tour so I knew I had two months to put paid to this Pearl White serial that had been flickering in my conscience for near on twenty years.

It was like writing a symphony in dribs and drabs. Three movements had been achieved with anguish, and now the final movement had to be brought forth with a suitable climax of exultation. I had to find the Nevinson and do something about the photographs I had taken of Barry.

The Humphries arrived in Sydney for the forthcoming tour. We were invited to the first night and attended the reception afterwards at the hotel where they were staying. There wasn't time for anything more than a wistful wave and a hurried hello as Barry was encircled by a crush of well-wishers. He gave a hurried acknowledgment whilst accepting felicitations gurgling from the corners of full mouths, stuffed with salmon, swimming in champagne. 'Phone me!' were the last words we heard as he was once more engulfed. So phone him I did and arrangements were made for them to have lunch with us.

After all the episodic frustrations I was determined to have everything ready for the handing-over ceremony which had so far escaped me. First, I searched for and found the Nevinson. Second, I made a selection of prints from various sessions I had had with him and third, I found all the negatives I had ever taken of him and transferred them onto a video tape, in a positive form. Some photographs were mounted, others bound into a small booklet and the lot packed into a box alongside the video tape. And of course, the Nevinson.

Barry regarded the box quizzically, then began the task of opening it with a look of concentrated anticipation, which gave way to an apparent joy, gratifying for me to see.

Vanessa Redgrave and Tariq Ali.

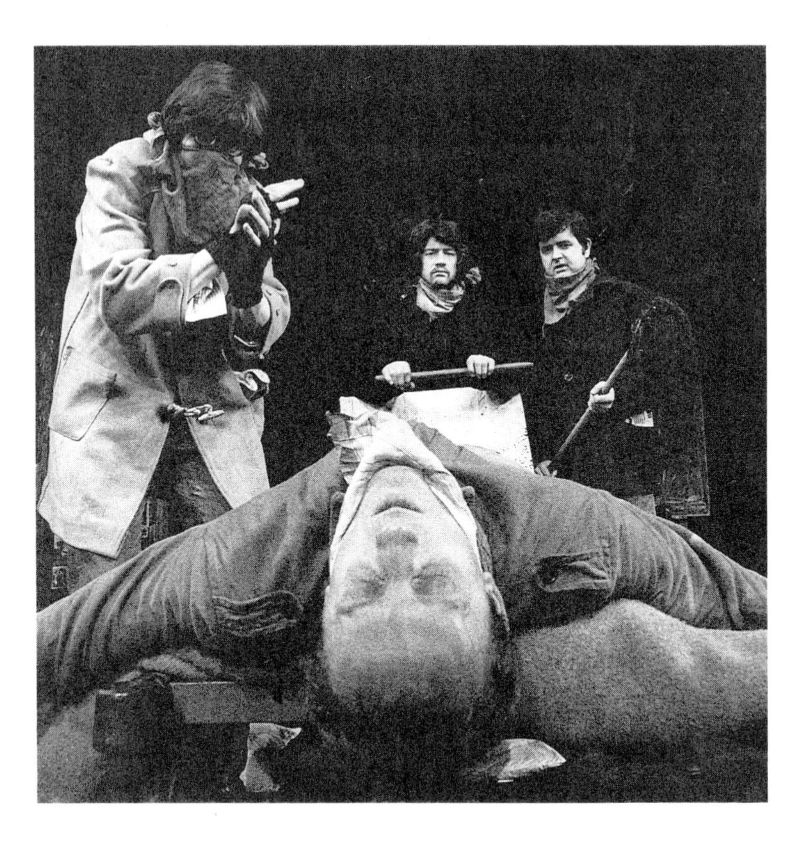

The cast of *Little Malcolm*, including John Hurt (*centre back stage*).

Cast members in *The Council of Love*.

Barry Humphries and camel (*top*). Ben Eriksson (*bottom*).

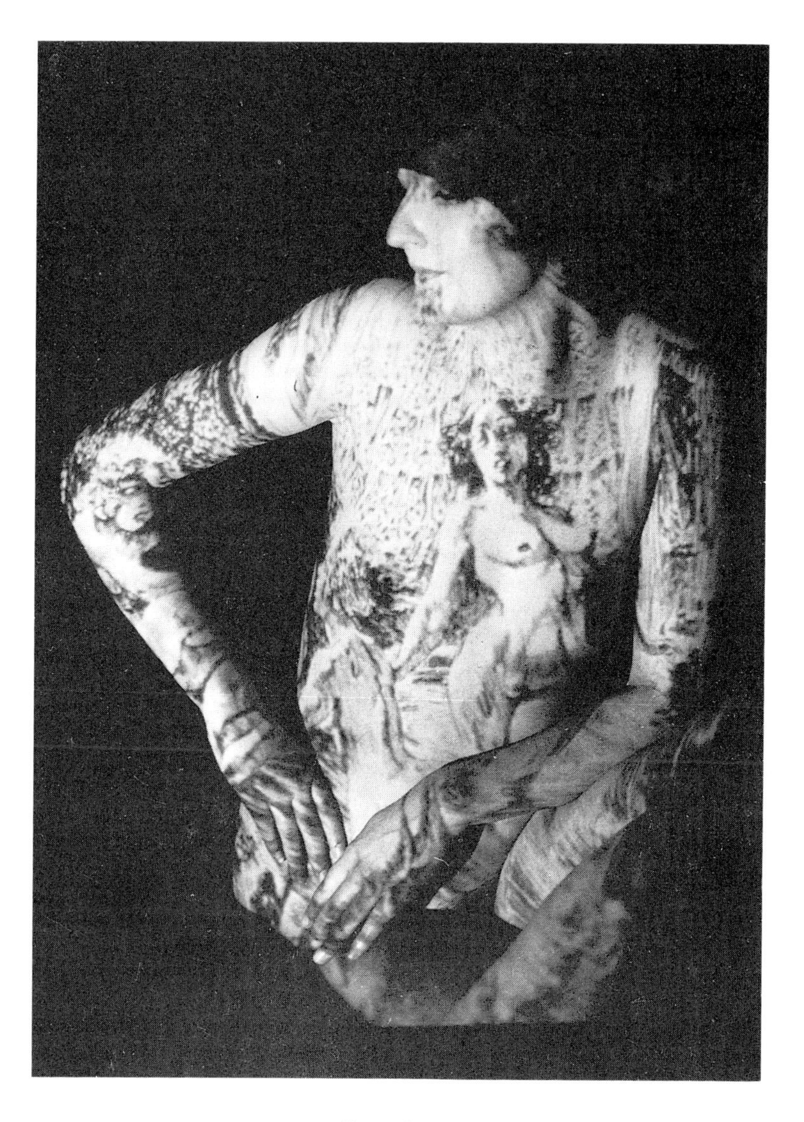

Helen Glad.

Lewis Morley, artist (*top*). Patricia Morley, subject (*bottom*).

Lloyd Rees, artist and Desiderius Orban.

'The lark descending'. Peter Carey 'snared' at his Surry Hills office, prior to his sitting for a portrait to be donated to the 'G'day Chair' AIDS Benefit Fund, 1991.

We spent a lot of the afternoon catching up on old friends and wondering where some of the faces that appeared in The National Portrait Gallery catalogue had disappeared to. One of the people we spoke of was a sixties friend, Roddy Maude-Roxby. I told Barry that Roddy had turned up at the opening of the exhibition and was still, as ever, the modest and talented actor that we had known from The Establishment days.

As they were leaving, Barry's attention was caught by a small, colour-reinforced pen and ink drawing. 'Lewis!' he exclaimed. 'You've got a Weitzer. I too have one...' He paused in his discovery and then said in a tone of wonderment. 'Do you realise Lewis that you and I are probably the only two people in Sydney, perhaps even in Australia, to each own a Weitzer and know Roddy Maude-Roxby?'

'Barry,' I replied. 'You are probably right!'

As they drove off I gave a last wave of goodbye and a final wave forever to a very large lump that detached itself from Christian and evaporated into the ether.

THE RECORDING ANGLE

not representing the sixties...

I don't like analysing photographs, I don't like analysing paintings. My whole attitude to life has been emotional and I depend on emotions to get my kicks. There are certain images that are great, like early Cartier Bresson, but I don't want to know anything more about them. Quite often one's reactions are coloured by knowing too much. We let our fantasies take over when we should tear them away. I always find myself resisting reading people's motivations for their work. It could so easily not be the truth. I'd rather just let the picture speak for itself. I relate to photographs and paintings purely on an emotional level. If they appeal to me, I can relate to them. If they're explained to me, I can appreciate them, but still not like them.

My attitude to the sixties was perhaps different to the attitudes that most people had. When one thinks of the sixties, one thinks of groups of people who liked a certain type of clothes, music and lifestyle. I don't represent the sixties. I didn't like the clothes, I didn't like the music, I didn't indulge in many aspects of the lifestyle. I represent only an angle on the sixties, someone who was watching from the sidelines, someone who was watching from the fringe.

Many of the people I photographed were only beginning on their careers when I photographed them, they had not yet become victims, or adepts of the cult of personality that has been promoted by the media in the intervening years. One lives out their lives in the media as if one is living out a truth, but it is the hype and publicity surrounding them that has created that truth.

I've never had the stamina or dedication to do the same thing over and over again. I get bored with things and then I want to go on to something else. One half of me wants to break out, while the other half...

judgments...

No matter who you are or what you are, if you get involved in a situation where your reputation depends on recognition, then it's very difficult not to let recognition take over from your abilities. If you are mediocre and you become elevated, at the back of your mind there's the fear. How *do* you judge yourself?

I know how good and how bad I am because I see the results. I know that many contemporary photographers are overestimated and I think photography itself is overestimated.

How does one judge a picture? Because of the Keeler picture I know that people will find much more merit in everything else I have done. If you have a photograph of a celebrity, you're three-quarters the way there. They are a known factor so one is dealing with something that has already attracted mass interest. I did work hard but I have had a constant battle with my ideas of what things are really worth.

the sixties...

I was there but I wasn't quite participating. I've always been like that. I jump in, then I jump out again. I don't really involve myself and that goes for everything I do.

Even my art collection reflects this. At one point, it's African, then pottery, then something else. I am not a true collector in that way. I lack stamina, I lack concentration and I lack dedication. I am not a dedicated person. I often feel that I would have liked to be dedicated to something but if I'm honest with myself then I realise that I've always held back.

I've seen so many friends who have been totally dedicated to what they do. If it's acting, then they talk, eat, sleep, dream acting, even if they're mediocre. I have known so many actors and actresses who are obsessed with theatre but when one goes to see their work, it's not particularly good. Their compensation comes from devoting all their energy to it.

The fear of mediocrity has always been there, with painting, even more than photography. So I have cultivated a habit of not taking any of it very seriously, of having safety nets, or escape routes through which I can escape criticism.

I could have gone back into commercial photography after the National Portrait Gallery show but I know my inadequacies, so I think: *Let it ride.*

confession is good for the soul but bad for the image...

The old adage that the camera never lies is the greatest lie of all. It is because of this that anyone who decides to take up reportage should beware of the dangerous current lurking beneath the surface.

I have always considered the camera a recording device and when used as such, as in the case of reportage, it must record. And to record is to tell the truth. Lenses, film, lighting conditions and circumstances all play a part in distorting the truth but all these pale beside that greatest lie of all, attitude. Not so much *how* you approach the subject matter but *why*. This is the question that only the photographer who took the picture can answer.

Time can blunt the original attitude and excuses can be offered for the act that produced the image, but behind every release of the shutter the reason *why* determines the validity of the result.

What is the greatest sin in this type of photography? Faking a shot. A lot of well-known photographs fall into this category of manufactured reality. The celebrated shot of the flag raising at Iwojima is one prime example. For me, such shots are the cardinal sins of photography but . . . and confession is good for the soul . . . I have been guilty of such faking myself.

It was while I was employed as a freelance photographer by Ned Sherrin to do all the stills on the BBC television program, 'That Was The Week That Was'. One of the segments of this ground-breaking weekly program was an exposé on lung cancer, 1963 style. I was commissioned to photograph a dead body and some cancerous lungs pitted by cigarette smoking, and arrangements had been made for me to shoot at the morgue where all the necessary images were housed under one roof.

The driver who took me there in the BBC car was anxious to accompany me inside as he had never seen a dead body and was eager to have this omission rectified. I found his desire macabre, to say the least, but didn't object as I thought he could assist me in the shoot. It was a fortuitous decision.

We were introduced to the doctor in charge who led us to the cold storage room where the cadavers were kept. They were in individual drawers that slid in and out of the wall that housed them, like a massive filing cabinet. The doctor slid out a tray that ran silently on its coasters, apologising that there was only this one body in the morgue at the moment. When he pulled back the white sheet that covered the corpse, he revealed the face of a woman, about sixty, very white, with excessively pink cheeks. Framing all

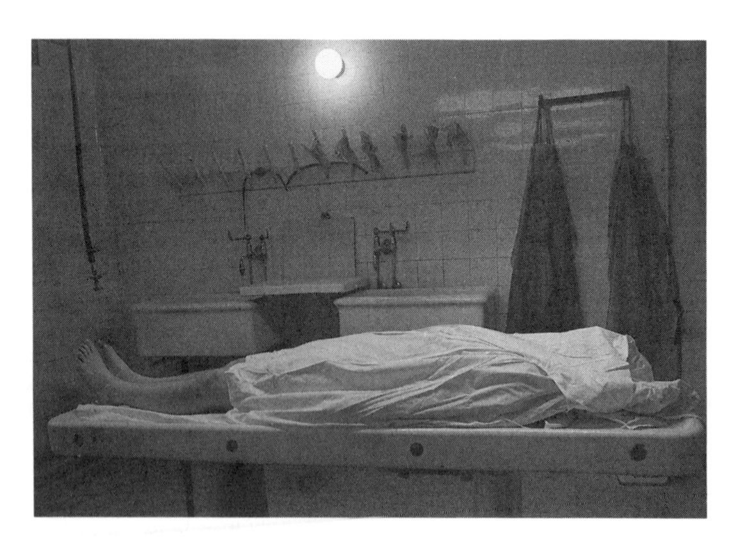

was an abundant coiffure of absolutely silver hair. It reminded me of a young child who had illicitly made use of mummy's make-up.

The doctor told us that her death had nothing to do with cancer and I was suddenly outraged that I had to photograph this situation, aware of my shame at disturbing the serenity of her sleep. I knew how unprofessional my reaction was but I felt I couldn't justify the indignity of trundling her to the slab in the dissection room just to get a photograph.

Yet I knew I had to come back with a picture of a dead person, lying on a slab in the mortuary, so I took the easy way out. I faked the shot.

I told the driver of my car to take off his trousers and lie on the slab while I photographed him, covered by a mortuary sheet. He thought it great fun, the doctor was amused by my squeamishness but I was ashamed of my professional cowardice. I justified my deceit by rationalising that even if I had used the dead woman, it would have been a fake as she had not died of lung cancer. We retired to the laboratory where some encrusted lungs were preserved in embalming fluid. They were the real McCoy. The whole affair rather shattered me and the first thing I did as I left the morgue and shakily clambered into the car was to light up a cigarette.

limited editions...

The other issue in photography that I have been rabidly opposed to, which raises the old argument of art versus camera (note I said camera, not photography) is the inflation of the value of a photograph by means of 'editions'.

Art, whatever that covers, and the camera, both exist. They are dead until life is given to them by a manipulator. The manipulations involving art are paintings, sculptures or works commonly known as 'art'. From the camera, there are photographs. The results then stand on their own merits.

I am not going to argue as to whether photography is art. Suffice to say that in my opinion it is not. To be more precise, if one must have labels, it is not fine art. But, to consisently take good photographs, one has to be an artist. A lot of famous photographers and thousands of less well-known ones have been frustrated, failed or just incompetent painters who have the vision but not the capacity to carry it out to their satisfaction. But they are artists nonetheless.

However, the claptrap of limited edition prints, scored through negatives and all the commercial hype invested in making the print more valuable through scarcity, is to me absolute anathema and not relevant to the role of a photograph. If people want numbers on their prints I am not averse to numbering and dating the prints consecutively, as they were personally printed by me.[2] My prayer is that collectors will get it into their heads that 'editioning' need not necessarily mean they hold one of a limited image. They might hold one of a limited image of that size. There is nothing to stop the photographer or dealer commissioning another printing of the same image on different paper, or of a different size, thus legally printing as many 'editions' as they deem fit. If photographs are to be collected, it should be for their aesthetic value, not their rarity.

exhumations...

I am like the duchess who never referred to her humble working-class origins, tending to bury some of the more shameful episodes of my career in the welter of later achievements. For instance, whenever the question is asked: 'Do you do passports? . . . or weddings? . . . or christenings?' I haughtily reply in the negative, but then am forced to admit that on one or two special, not to be repeated occasions, I have committed these heinous acts.

2. Contrary to my instructions, two of my images have been issued as 'editions'—an irreversible fait accompli.

Let me exhume these memories, air them, and hope to regain some of the Persil whiteness that was once in evidence, rather than the dingy grey that has resulted from secrecy.

Only months ago I dug out the negatives of a joint christening which I photographed. The prints were never delivered to the parents of the children involved for the simple reason that I never did any, in spite of repeated requests from the disappointed parties. The two babies in question were relatively close to me, in fact, one was my own son. It was easy enough to fob off those intimately at hand, and soon, enquiries from the other quarter also ceased. Finally, when I found time to do the prints and sent one batch to their rightful owner, she nearly swooned in disbelief. The other batch I handed to my wife who was equally dumbfounded. My son, you see, was by now 34 years old!

Two sets of wedding negatives also testify to my lapses: those of my sister's wedding which I lost before my prints were made and those belonging to another long-lost London friend. And yes, I plead guilty too, to the further charge of having knowingly consorted with that lowest form of photograph [illegible] eproduction, the passport photograph.

It was while I was working for The National Theatre that I received an urgent phone call from Virginia Fairweather, its public relations officer, asking for a favour with which I reluctantly complied.

The entire cast and crew were off to Russia. Many of the better known and well-travelled strolling thespians were armed with the key that unlocked the doors to foreign travel, but many of the underlings were lacking a valid passport. One of the prerequisites for this essential document was a photograph. Along with Angus McBean, I was at the time engaged in photographing their current productions for front-of-house and publicity. It was deemed that I would be cheaper than the Master himself, even should he consider doing so menial a task.

So there I was, backstage at the theatre with a straight-backed wooden chair placed between two floodlights borrowed from the array of lighting equipment that was strewn around the wings. The camera was poised, ready to start snapping the ever increasing snake line of people who were impatiently waiting to get back to their duties.

Michael Gambon

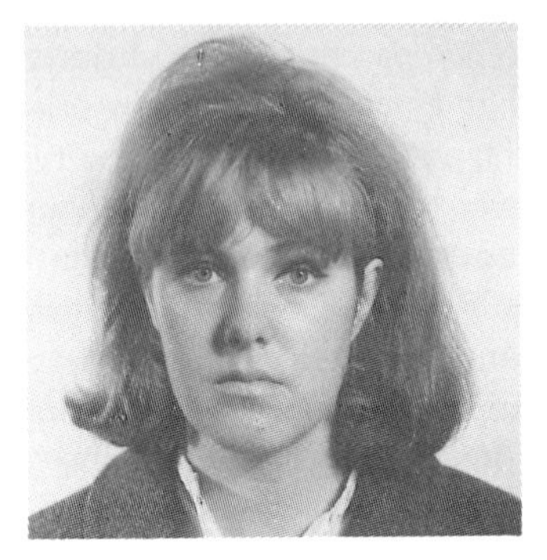

Lyn Redgrave

Mixed amongst the stagehands and other technical crew were some actors who are now household names. Among them were Frank Finlay, Michael Gambon, Lyn Redgrave and Joan Plowright and the lighting director, Richard Piltbrow.

'Fancy having my passport photo taken by Lewis Morley!' quipped Richard.

'Shut up, or I'll make you do your own lighting,' I replied.

As I look at my proof-sheets for the job I'm forced to admit it was not the happiest of occasions. Indeed, I may perhaps have broken the record for the largest group of dissatisfied sitters at one session.

the recording angle...

I've always wanted to record things, usually the better things in life, while sweeping the less desirable under the carpet. Perhaps the desire to avoid facing the future, or even the present creates the urge to record, to retain the image of the frozen moment. It is concrete proof that one has been there, done that. It shores up one's frail determination to face the future, a prospect easier to face by looking back.

I have always loved travel, recording the journey with camera and sketch pad, increasing the enjoyment of the experience... except when the trip happens to be an assignment. Then there is responsibility—one must return with the goods. It becomes a chore. That is why I have never travelled to photograph a job on 'spec'. It would be a self-defeating exercise.

All my commissioned trips have had one thing in common—knots in the stomach. I start worrying about the people I will be letting down if I don't return with the desired results. In a way, I'm glad it is all over. I don't want to take photographs for other people.

I have spent most of my life in a love–hate relationship with photography. It has been a life filled with emotion and some of the greatest joys and greatest traumas have been related to photography.

Yes, I wanted to be a painter but I know that even if I had been a successful one, I would never have experienced the very full life that I have enjoyed through picking up a camera, instead of paints and a brush.

Also published in Imprint Lives

Wards of the State: An Autobiographical Novella

Robert Adamson

She sat on the mudguard and let her hair roll forward; black hair fell down her face, but she didn't care abut the screaming going on all around her. She just wanted to keep moving, to get back into the car and go. Anywhere, what did it matter, as long as the road hissed behind her.

Robert Adamson's autobiography is a poetic evocation of his childhood and boyhood in Sydney and on the Hawkesbury River. It encompasses the teenage dreams — girls, cars and impending manhood — which drew him into the closed net of boys' homes and a criminal life. Adamson finds in writing both release and resolution.

'Adamson is probably the best lyric poet in the country.
He can write about the natural world more convincingly than anyone else. But at the same time Adamson is completely contemporary in his verse technique.
He is a sort of feral Mallarmé.'
John Forbes, *Melbourne Herald*

Brett Whiteley
Sandra McGrath

Art should astonish, transmute, transfix. One must work at the tissue between truth and paranoia.

The art of painting ... always has been and always will be a game. The rules of the game are quite simple: in a given arena, on as many psychic fronts as the talents allow, one must visually describe the centre of the meaning of existence.

Brett Whiteley

Brett Whiteley was undoubtedly one of Australia's most astonishing and prolific artists. This book provides a general summary of Whiteley's work and illustrates the diversity of subject, style and technique used by the artist throughout his life.

Sandra McGrath was closely associated with the artist and his family and gives an intimate insight into Whiteley's character, and the circumstances and events which influenced and inspired him. Through excerpts from informal conversations, taped interviews and extracts from his diaries, she has largely let Whiteley's own voice tell his story.

Peggy Glanville-Hicks

Wendy Beckett

In 1932, at the age of nineteen, Peggy Glanville-Hicks left Australia for London and the Royal College of Music, determined on a career as a composer. There she studied with Ralph Vaughan Williams, and graduated with a prestigious travelling scholarship to continue her composition studies. But as a woman she had to struggle to be taken on by Nadia Boulanger, for though a woman herself, Boulanger feared that life as a composer faced women with more difficulties than pleasures.

Peggy Glanville-Hicks' life was not without difficulties or pleasures, and this biography traces both — through her troubled marriage to the homosexual composer Stanley Bate, through an erratic but ultimately dazzling career, through friendship and illness, and her years living in America, and in Greece.

In writing this biography, Wendy Beckett has interviewed friends of Peggy Glanville-Hicks, including Leonard Bernstein, and her lover Paul Bowles. In telling her compelling story, the biographer has brought to life the witty and eccentric woman whose work included the operas *Nausicaa* and *The Transposed Heads*, as well as *The Masque of the Wild Man* and *Three Gymnopedie*.